The
Essential Guide to

GP EMERGENCIES

The
Essential Guide to

GP EMERGENCIES

Judith Fisher MB BS FRCGP

MAGISTER CONSULTING LTD

Published in the UK by
Magister Consulting Ltd
The Old Rectory
St. Mary's Road
Stone
Dartford
Kent DA9 9AS

Copyright © 2001 Magister Consulting Ltd
First published 1999 by Magister Consulting Ltd
Reprinted 2001, 2002
Printed in Italy by Fotolito Longo Group

ISBN 1 873839 15 4

This publication reflects the views and experience of the author and not necessarily those of Magister Consulting Ltd.

Any product mentioned in this book should be used in accordance with the prescribing information prepared by the manufacturer. Neither the author nor the publisher can accept responsibility for any detrimental consequences arising from the information contained herein. Dosages given are for guidance purposes only. No sanctions or endorsements are made for any drug or compound at present under clinical investigation.

ABOUT THE AUTHOR

Dr Judith Fisher is a Consultant in Accident and Emergency, formerly responsible for primary care at The Royal Hospital's NHS Trust, and Honorary Senior Lecturer in General Practice. This was the first such appointment in the UK. The post was established to improve communications between the accident and emergency department and the community and to provide a GP-type response to those patients who present with problems more suitably dealt with in primary care. She currently works at Princess Alexandra Hospital. Before entering hospital practice she had been a general practitioner for 30 years, active in immediate care and major incident management.

Dr Fisher was founder chairman of the Resuscitation Council (UK), a past chairman of the British Association for Immediate Care (BASICS) and is now an examiner for The Diploma in Immediate Medical Care and a member of the Football Licensing Authority. She is involved in pre-hospital care and, following Lord Justice Taylor's report into the Hillsborough tragedy, has been running courses for doctors involved in mass-gathering medicine. As the immediate past secretary of The World Association for Disaster and Emergency Medicine she has been involved in international educational initiatives. Dr Fisher now enjoys her role as joint honorary secretary to the Joint Colleges and Ambulance Liaison committee where she has a further opportunity to work collaboratively with the ambulance service in looking at future developments. In her leisure time she is a busy grandmother to seven grandchildren and enjoys gardening and entertaining.

This book is dedicated to my dear friend and mentor, the most selfless general practitioner I know, the founder of Immediate Care and The Founder Chairman of BASICS - Dr Kenneth Easton OStJ OBE

CONTENTS

FOREWORD

Emergency care forms a relatively small part of the workload of general practitioners, and is of disproportionate importance for patients and doctors. This results from patients' most urgent needs, including life-threatening situations, and is understandably surrounded by anxiety and sometimes fear. For doctors, it can tax the skills of the generalist to the utmost, both in terms of clinical judgement and the situations in which problems present themselves.

The organisational context in which emergency work is carried out is changing. The emergence of general practitioner co-operatives, the changing pattern of home visiting, and the shifting interface between primary and secondary care are all having a significant impact. The place of accident and emergency departments and the role of nursing colleagues in the provision of emergency care are all under review and may change significantly as a result. At the same time, training for general practitioners and nursing colleagues is in a state of flux. While the changes promise more appropriate education, this has yet to emerge.

In any situation, a book which both sets the scene and offers a wealth of advice is extremely welcome. Judith Fisher has managed to draw on her unique experience of providing and studying emergency care to bring together a comprehensive text which will offer those providing emergency care and those who are in training a source of information and advice. This book is highly recommended to general practitioners and nursing colleagues who may be involved in emergency care, and should find a place in the libraries of practices and other emergency care providers.

Dr John Toby
Chairman of Council RCGP

USEFUL LOCAL TELEPHONE NUMBERS

Out-of-hours nurses and midwives..

Local hospital..

Ambulance service (doctor's designated line)...................................

Emergency social worker..

Crisis intervention team ....

Bereavement counsellor ....

Local police station(s)...

Coroner's officer ....

Local funeral directors ....

Parish priest, rabbi or mullah...

Duty midwife ....

Local Health Authority emergency number...

National Poisons Information Service

National...

Regional..

Samaritans and any self-help organisations.......................................

....

....

OTHER USEFUL LOCAL TELEPHONE NUMBERS

....

....

....

....

....

....

....

....

....

....

....

....

....

....

1 GENERAL INFORMATION

GENERAL INFORMATION ABOUT

THE EMERGENCY WORKLOAD

IN GENERAL PRACTICE

Some guidance on telephone advice

Our allies the ambulance service

The doctor's bag and in-car equipment

The unconscious patient

GENERAL INFORMATION

Only 5% of people who contact their doctor out-of-hours in a typical suburban practice area are admitted to hospital. Fifteen per cent of all adults attending the accident and emergency department are referred by their GPs, while two-thirds of patients attending will be self-referred, often by dialling 999[1]. The patient's perception of what is an emergency is very different from those in the profession.

More and more GPs are working in large groups or co-operatives and so will be seeing patients whose medical history is unfamiliar to them. Protocols are being jointly devised between purchasers and providers, with politicians suggesting they may set national treatment protocols as part of managed care[2]. Evidenced-based medicine is leading to appropriate district and national protocols which should guide your care, rather than cost or political agenda.

In 1996, there were 28,869 general practitioners in the UK with an average list size of 1887 patients, of which 16% were aged over 65 years[3]. These GPs will make major decisions on emergency management within their Primary Care Trusts. The majority of GP's workload is amazingly similar, falling between narrow medians. In 1992, the annual consultation rate (mainly at the surgery) averaged 3-4 consultations per patient per year (Range 1-6). At that time the telephone played little part in the consultation process, although in Scandinavian countries it already accounted for 30-40% of patient contacts. At the time of these figures health promotion was just beginning to influence patient appointments, with the estimated workload caused by health promotion and prevention rising from 5% to 15%.

Night visits represented only a small part of the GP's work (38 per year per GP), while consultations and home visits took up 68% of doctors time, though the number of emergency calls by day was not calculated. However, from my own 30 years in practice, we had one to two 'late' calls per day, which came in-between the distribution of visits at 11am and the evening-duty doctor's shift. These calls were usually to the chronically ill (with an exacerbation picked up by a visiting nurse or relative), to a child, or to acute psychiatric emergencies. Whereas the former two calls were usually fairly straightforward, the latter were not. Their infrequency was far outweighed by the anxiety and disruption caused. As GP workload increases the disruption caused by these calls becomes more evident.

From the work by the late John Fry[4] we see that a doctor with a list of 2000 patients would have an annual incidence of 116 cases of acute bronchitis, 12 cases of pneumonia (no mention of asthma), eight patients with acute myocardial infarction, four sudden deaths and six cases of acute stroke. Of those with psychiatric illness there would be 10 with severe depression, four parasuicides and one suicide every four years. On the surgical side, there would be six acute abdominal disorders needing surgery (and many more who did not).

3

Against this background, the family practitioner needs to be competent in coping with emergencies and be aware of who else from the community is available to help. It is increasingly common for the doctor to work with an ambulance crew in order to provide the best care for a patient. Frequently a decision is made jointly between the community and hospital teams concerning the best management of conditions. For instance, they would advise that a patient with chest pain should summon an ambulance and go straight to the hospital rather than call his family doctor. It is a debate that will continue, with the response varying from area to area. The important issue is that a decision has been made and this decision is known to the community, the hospital and practice teams, so that correct advice is given at all times.

Telephone helplines are already used both formally and informally. In developing such helplines, local treatment protocols developed between hospital and community services should be used, rather than purchasing overseas systems unsuited to the UK (such as 'Ask A Nurse' from USA). Those developed by the Primary Care Unit at King's College Hospital are an example of good practice. Within our practices, telephone calls are usually taken by reception staff who need guidelines on telephone procedure and on how to recognise emergencies. They should also have very clear instructions on how to contact a doctor if one is not on the premises.

Several reviews of hospital and ambulance service telephone triage/decision-support systems are available through the Ambulance Service Association and NHSE (such as that undertaken by Professor Nichol and his team at Sheffield). It is not the review that is needed so much as the government desire to implement the recommendations.

A comprehensive nationwide telephone triage and helpline is being piloted by the Department of Health. Patients dialling 888 will be given health advice by trained nurses or paramedics, in an attempt to reduce visits to hospital or the GP. Here, we are looking at how to cope with the patient who feels he has an urgent condition; how to tease out the essential information to allow us to decide when to visit, and what to do thereafter in order to provide both patient and doctor satisfaction in an increasingly busy health service.

Finally, when the doctor goes to visit or treat an emergency patient, he must remember the law and the meaning of informed consent. Failure to get the patient's consent to any examination or treatment leaves the doctor open to a charge of assault. If the patient is unable to give consent, because they have a mental impairment (either through unconsciousness, confusion or a psychiatric condition), then only treatment necessary to prevent death or deterioration, administered

in the patient's interest, should be given. It is even more important to keep accurate contemporaneous notes in such circumstances and, if present, obtain the relatives agreement to your actions. Do not be persuaded by relatives to overstep this boundary, for instance when relatives request inappropriate sedation or analgesia for the disturbed or wandering patient.

SOME GUIDANCE ON TELEPHONE ADVICE

More and more frequently patients are receiving telephone advice from their GP, commercial advice lines and the ambulance service. Provided the caller is happy with that advice and will call again if the situation changes, this is one method of dealing with out-of-hours calls which are an 'emergency' to the patient. A few ground rules may help to keep you out of trouble.

Because the patient is not in front of you and there are no 'body language' clues accompanying the conversation, pay particular attention to the emotional content of the dialogue. Obtain accurate and complete information from the caller, and check that they have understood the subsequent advice. It is convenient to consider the telephone consultation in five stages.

The five stages of a telephone consultation

- ☑ Introduction
- ☑ Listening
- ☑ Clarifying
- ☑ Advising
- ☑ Safety net

During the **introduction** make sure the patient is aware of your identity and you are clear to whom you are talking - patient, relative or friend. Introduce yourself, if you are returning a call taken by a receptionist, and ensure you have all the patient details. If you are working for a co-operative or commercial deputising service which records the telephone calls, advise the patient of this and explain that this is to help reduce misunderstandings and audit patient care.

Listen carefully to the spoken story and identify any underlying messages. Acknowledge the patient's or relative's concerns, checking back in an encouraging way. For instance: *'You sound worried. Is anything in particular worrying you?'*. Let the patient tell the story and make notes. **Clarify** the key points by asking, for example, *'Now let me see if I have this all clear, you say that...'* Allow time to give a complete history.

When you are both sure the situation has been explained clearly, move on to give **advice**. Give this in small chunks, checking the caller has understood. Speak clearly and avoid jargon. Check your pace and ask if the patient is following you. Avoid

being patronising; you will know what pace the patient can take after a few phrases. Ensure the caller understands what has been said; encourage them to repeat the advice and to write it down. Be specific about what to look for or expect. Finally, invite questions and ask if there is anything else. Ensure the caller feels you have done all they expected and check how they feel about the decisions. It is helpful to say that calling for advice was the correct thing to do and suggest they call again if concerned or if there is a deterioration in the patient's condition **(safety net)**.

Good telephone advice is an essential tool in the management of emergency patients, provided it is used appropriately for the patient's benefit and not to reduce the doctor's workload. Recording all calls is a helpful way of auditing your telephone manner and is also useful for subsequent enquiries or complaints. A contemporaneous recording is acceptable as legal evidence should a case ever come to court.

OUR ALLIES THE AMBULANCE SERVICE

The United Kingdom has an ambulance service which is the envy of the world. It is integrated into the health service nationwide with a universal training programme and a single access number. Since the early 1950s, when the service provided transport with very basic first-aid, it has developed into a highly professional care delivery system, with patient-transport and accident-and-emergency divisions. Since the advent of ambulance trusts and the search for income generation, many services have developed stronger links with their local family doctors, providing message and pager services, full answering and advice services for co-operatives, and training programmes for doctors and their practice staff in basic and advanced life support.

All emergency calls are dealt with according to strict protocols. Doctors' lines will be answered by a telephone control-room assistant who has a set list of questions that must be asked, so do not rush to bypass the system. It may seem a long process but only takes less than a minute. These protocols ('*Criteria-Based Despatch*' or '*Medical Priority Despatch*') aim to alert the appropriate type of response to each situation, whoever calls the service. A patient presenting with chest pain or with difficulty in breathing elicits an immediate response, whereas a patient with back pain may have to wait six months. Unfortunately, the government did not accept a recent review concerning recommendations[5] that some calls could be suitably referred elsewhere rather than wasted on valuable ambulance resources.

The accident and emergency side of the service is delivered by paramedics and ambulance technicians. Before moving on to the operational issues and ambulance aid, the ambulance technician training starts with an introduction which concentrates on professional behaviour. This section concentrates on

non-emergency patients first, where the initial training begins, allowing the new recruit to practise his communication skills, his patient handling, and liaison with base and hospital. The emergency section of the training looks at the overall assessment of a patient and the scene. This is broken into six sections.

Assessment of patient and scene

1 Survey of the emergency scene
   (either in the street or the patient's home).

2 Approach.

3 The primary patient survey,
   resuscitation if required.

4 Secondary survey with a closer look at
   everything, including a comprehensive history.

5 Patient management and transport.

6 Reassessment before the final pre-alert stage,
   where the medical facility is notified of the
   patient's condition.

The medical facility is usually the local hospital, but may be the general practitioner if the crew feels the patient does not warrant immediate transport to hospital.

Only after becoming familiar with this generic approach does today's technician go on to look at the body and its structure, including simple cellular biology and tissue function, the meaning of basic anatomical terms, and the components and boundaries of the body cavities. Over the rest of the course the various systems are covered, both from the physiological and pathological processes seen and the management of common conditions. For example, the respiratory system covers the components and function of the respiratory system, the composition of inspired and expired air, the mechanics of ventilation and the mechanism and management of respiratory arrest. It divides chest disease into airway obstruction (bronchitis, emphysema and asthma), impaired perfusion (pneumonia, pleurisy and pulmonary embolism), and industrial lung disease (silicosis, pneumoconiosis, byssinosis and asbestosis). Chest injury and examination of the injured chest follow a logical sequence in an attempt to ensure the detection of fractured ribs, pneumothoraces, and finishing with the different types of drowning and hypothermia.

The circulatory, skeletal, nervous and digestive systems are taught in a similar manner, followed by soft-tissue injuries, diabetes, poisoning and extremes of body temperature. There are separate sections on maternity, infants and children, mental illness, haemodialysis, infectious diseases (including HIV and AIDS) as well as special circumstances: major incidents, chemical or nuclear events, civil disturbance and handling violence, the law and ambulance staff, the management of bodies, and suspected death.

All this training does not mean the technician can now manage patients alone, but he has a core of knowledge allowing him to

be a competent assistant to his paramedic colleague. Kenneth Clarke's aim to have a paramedic on every front-line ambulance by December 1995 has been difficult to obtain in some areas, but a paramedic is despatched to 999 calls whenever possible. The technician is taught to assist the paramedic in selected procedures: airway management and intubation, intravenous access, cardiac monitoring and defibrillation, together with drug administration.

Many services offer additional skills to the competent ambulance technician before he is eligible to enter a paramedic training programme. The most popular programme is the one on defibrillation, which has been adopted by most trusts in an attempt to reduce deaths from cardiac arrest. Other skills (subject to local variation) undertaken as 'stand alone' modules include nebuliser use in the asthmatic patient, and catheterisation. In some areas, ambulance services are basing vehicles at hospital accident and emergency departments, where the technicians can be of help while awaiting calls, and in other areas they are placed strategically throughout the area.

After at least 12 months on an accident and emergency (sometimes called a front-line) ambulance, a technician can consider applying for selection to enter the paramedic training programme. Since personality and temperament are so important, nobody reaches the selection panel without a recommendation from his/her station officer or supervisor.

The three-stage programme starts with a week of basic anatomy and physiology followed by four weeks further theoretical and practical training. This clinical programme includes practical skills in endotracheal intubation, intravenous access, ECG monitoring and defibrillation together with drug administration.

Once this school work is completed, the potential paramedic spends time on a hospital attachment with anaesthesia, cardiology and intensive care departments, as well as some work in accident and emergency. This is stage three, which aims for the trainee to achieve competence within the clinical setting using those techniques developed during stage two.

The paramedic training covers more than knowledge and skills; there is a stress on attitude both toward patients and the medical profession. Trainees are encouraged to remember tact; there is a good phrase in one of the training manuals:

*'Recognising medical supremacy
is the best way to avoid conflict!'*

At times this must be hard when a medical practitioner appears on the scene and attempts to take over in an environment completely alien to his normal habitat.

Some services offer additional paramedic skills, such as needle thoracostomy, interosseous infusion, 12-lead ECG interpretation and a drug module. However, the general practitioner should assume that even though a paramedic has undertaken the national course, perhaps he has not used his skills too

frequently since then. Although he may be a competent technician, his clinical knowledge is not broad and tends to be protocol-driven. The sick patient is often best served by the doctor and ambulance staff working together, with the doctor providing a management overview and additional skills, such as opiate analgesia, while the technical procedures are performed by the paramedic assisted by his colleague.

THE DOCTOR'S BAG AND IN-CAR EQUIPMENT

Drugs

It is sensible to develop a practice formulary in conjunction with community and hospital colleagues. Evidenced-based medicine is leading to rational shared-management protocols. Your local hospital bacteriology department will work closely with the pharmacy to ensure there is an appropriate district antibiotic policy. Many doctors feel it is inappropriate to carry unfamiliar drugs that are used infrequently. Respiratory arrest can be treated with exhaled air resuscitation, bag valve mask or oxygen. However, if a doctor is going to carry opiates for the relief of stress and pain, he would be negligent not to carry naloxone.

Analgesics

Diamorphine powder 5 mg or 10 mg per vial

Morphine tartrate 10 mg with 50 mg cyclizine in 1ml

Diclofenac sodium 75 mg in 3 ml vial and 50 mg tablets

Naloxone 400 micrograms in 1 ml Opiate antagonists

Antibiotics

Amoxycillin as syrup, caps and dispersible

Co-amoxiclav 375 mg caps

Erythromycin ethyl succinate tabs 500 mg and paediatric sachets

Metronidazole 400 mg

Penicillin G 600 mg powder per vial x 2

Tetracyclines, e.g. doxycycline and oxytetracycline

Trimethoprim 200 mg

Antiemetics

Prochlorperazine 12.5 mg/ml vial and 5 mg suppositories

Metoclopramide 10 mg/2 ml vial

Cardiac drugs

Adrenaline 1:10,000 10 ml in pre-prepared syringe x 2

Adrenaline 1:1,000 in 1 ml x 2

Aspirin dispersible 300 mg

Atropine sulphate 3 mg and 0.5 mg pre-filled syringes x 2

Frusemide injection 10 mg/ml in 2 ml vial

Glyceryl trinitrate (GTN) spray

Lignocaine 100 mg in 100 ml

Benzodiazepines

Diazepam, tablets 2 mg or 5 mg, rectal 10 mg
in pre-prepared vial for adults, ampules 10 mg

Flumazenil 500 micrograms in 5 ml vials

Benzodiazepine antagonists

Bronchodilators

Aminophylline 250 mg vials for IV use

Eye preparations

Fluorescein (fluorets or minims)

Pilocarpine single dose

Tropicamide individual dose

Adrenaline (EPPY) single dose

Nebules

Salbutamol

Ipatropium bromide

Neuroleptics

Chlorpromazine tablets 25 mg

Haloperidol injection 10 mg/ml in 2 ml vials

Thioridazine suspension 100 mg/5 ml

Steroids

Hydrocortisone sodium succinate 100 mg powder
with separate diluent

Prednisolone soluble tablets 5 mg

Dexamethasone 4 mg/ml, 2 ml vials

Budesonide for nebuliser

Paediatric preparations

Paracetamol suspension 120 mg/5 ml

Ibuprofen suspension 100 mg/5 ml

Codeine phosphate oral solution 25 mg/5 ml

Rectal solution of diazepam, 5 mg in solution

Oral rehydration sachets

Paediatric suspension of phenoxymethyl penicillin, amoxycillin, trimethoprim, erythromycin and co-amoxiclav

Sterile saline sachets to dilute drugs to more convenient volumes

Other useful drugs

Chlorpheniramine 10 mg/ml vial

Dextrose 50 mg in 50 ml pre-filled syringe

Phenytoin ampules 50 mg/ml in 5 ml vials

Procyclidine injection 5 mg/ml, 2 ml vial

Propranolol injection 1 mg/ml

Contents of diagnostic bag

Stethoscope

Sphygmomanometer

Thermometer - normal and low reading

Peak flow monitor with spare mouthpieces

Auriscope/ophthalmoscope with spare earpieces

Snellen chart

Cotton buds

Fine blunt forceps (to remove foreign body from eye)

Tuning fork

Nasal speculae and nasal/aural long forceps

Tongue depressors

'Broslow' tape

Small toy

Blood sugar reagent sticks

Uristix

Sterile swabs and media

Blood and urine sample bottles

Sterile and disposable gloves

Resuscitation bag

Laerdal pocket mask with oxygen port

Oropharyngeal airways

Syringes and range of needles

Butterfly or other cannulae and plasters

Giving sets and fluid as appropriate
(two crystalloid, two colloid)

Pre-packed cardiac arrest drugs from drug list

Single items of equipment

Oxygen cylinder with plastic tubing and face mask

Nebuliser and/or nebuliser attachments

Consider - defibrillator and nitrous oxide 50% / oxygen 50%

Paperwork

Record cards

Prescription pads

Referral forms or writing paper

Section 2 and 4 forms (Mental Health Act)

Maps including those of new estates

Asthma chart

Patient advice sheets

Reference books - BNF or local formulary

GENERAL INFORMATION

THE UNCONSCIOUS PATIENT

This is one of the most common problems in general practice and covers a wide range of situations, from the deaf patient having a quiet doze, through to death. A system of assessment and response should be almost automatic. In victims of diabetes, poisoning, cardiac or respiratory failure, or any other condition, the response is identical. All require a 'quick-look' assessment, while evaluating and stabilising the **ABC** -

> **A**irway
>
> **B**reathing
>
> **C**irculation

- before a rapid assessment of the level of consciousness (**D** for disability in the alphabetical sequence), then a secondary survey to elucidate the precipitating factors. In cases of trauma the **A** is combined with cervical spine control.

History
If simple questioning of a telephone caller cannot clarify an easily reversible cause, the ambulance service should be alerted at the same time as you prepare to visit. All that is needed initially is information concerning breathing and circulation; if there is doubt that neither is present, move at once. Only after establishing their presence should you continue to assess

Disability by determining the level of responsiveness. **AVPU** -

Alert, responding to

Verbal commands, responding to

Painful stimuli, or

Unrouseable

- is sufficient for the initial assessment.

Again, the level of response determines whether you visit immediately or continue to gather information. If the patient seems to be responding to verbal stimuli, there is time to focus further on the underlying disease process. Student mnemonics seem to stay fixed in one's mind.

TIN MEN DECEIVE TB ensures you cover the various aetiologies of different disease manifestations in a difficult case -

Traumatic

Infective

Neurological

Metabolic

Endocrine

Neoplastic

Drugs

Congenitial

Vascular

TB

-although frequently the cause is obvious.

Examination of the unconscious patient
Unconsciousness covers a range of neurodisability. Although the AVPU quick-look assessment is ideal in the initial phase, the Glasgow Coma Scale (GCS - *see Figure One*) is the measure

used to identify the grade of coma. It tests three levels of response: Eye opening, best motor response and verbal response. Each are given a score and the total of the three scores is the GCS[6]. This can be monitored at regular intervals to give a numerical guide to improvement or deterioration. It is a scale incorporated into most ambulance report forms and accident and emergency department notes. Specific aspects of background, history, diagnosis and management for different conditions are discussed below.

Management

While searching for a cause, the generic approach is the ABC of resuscitation as required, so **MOVE** -

Monitor

Oxygen

Venous access

Evaluate

CARDIAC ARREST

This is the final common pathway for death in the community. This is usually due to primary cardiac disease. Its management is the same, whatever the cause.

(see section on Cardiovascular Emergencies p.39)

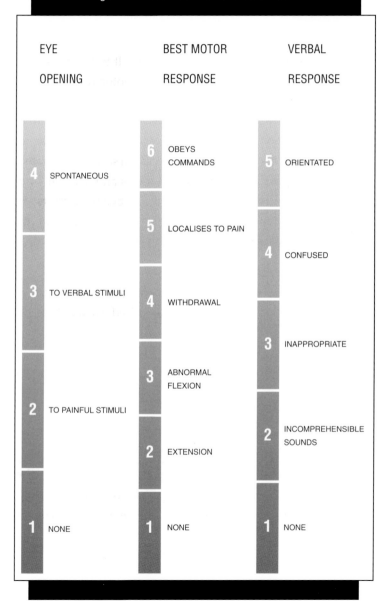

Figure One: **THE GLASGOW COMA SCALE**

EYE OPENING

4 SPONTANEOUS
3 TO VERBAL STIMULI
2 TO PAINFUL STIMULI
1 NONE

BEST MOTOR RESPONSE

6 OBEYS COMMANDS
5 LOCALISES TO PAIN
4 WITHDRAWAL
3 ABNORMAL FLEXION
2 EXTENSION
1 NONE

VERBAL RESPONSE

5 ORIENTATED
4 CONFUSED
3 INAPPROPRIATE
2 INCOMPREHENSIBLE SOUNDS
1 NONE

GENERAL INFORMATION

TRAUMA

Background

Since the unconscious patient is unable to give a history, try to question a bystander while starting your initial assessment. The most common cause of unconsciousness after an accident is head injury, though always be aware that a preceding medical crisis may have caused the accident (myocardial infarction being the most common). Alternatively, the patient may be exsanguinating from both overt and covert blood loss.

INFECTION

Although septic shock usually presents with a flushed and confused or unconscious patient who is hypotensive, oliguric and febrile, the condition progresses to a pre-terminal phase of normal- or low-core temperature with peripheral shutdown. You may see the purpuric rash of disseminated intravascular coagulation which can be confused with meningococcal septicaemia *(Infectious Diseases and Rashes p.163)*. Always have a high index of suspicion for this condition with the unconscious patient in whom a cause has not been found. Immunocompromised and immunosuppressed patients are particularly at risk, as early symptoms may be masked. Diabetic patients with septicaemia may go into a metabolic acidosis *(see p.29)*.

The most common infective cause of unconsciousness world-wide must be the malarial parasite, but in the UK this is only likely in immigrant communities and travellers, particularly from the sub-Saharan regions of Africa or southeast Asia. Always take a travel history and consider tropical diseases with those at risk. Remember to ask where the air traveller's flights stopped to re-fuel, as insect-borne diseases have been caught on stopovers.

The mortality of septic shock is 50%. Patients should be transferred to hospital rapidly. Oxygen should be administered, along with an IV infusion of crystalloid if there is going to be any delay in transfer or a long journey is expected. If meningo-coccal meningitis is suspected, give penicillin IV 1200 mg before the patient is moved to hospital. (Ceftriaxone is now recommended as the first-line antibiotic for use in hospitals, but it is not usual to have this medication in general practice except in the case of an epidemic.)

NEUROLOGICAL *(see also Neurological Emergencies p.131)*

This group provides the most frequent causes of unconscious-ness met as emergencies in general practice. Semantically, all unconscious patients are a neurological emergency, but here we consider those with a primary cause in the nervous system, for instance, those who experience fits or sudden neurological deficit.

GENERAL INFORMATION

EPILEPTIC FITS *(see also Neurological Emergencies p.132)*

The patient who is unconscious following a fit will usually recover spontaneously, but if there is an underlying cause to be reversed, recovery is delayed. Undertake the ABCs of resuscitation, and control the fit before seeking the cause. Status epilepticus (a fit that lasts for over 10 minutes or recurrent fits without full recovery in between each episode) will lead to permanent brain damage due to hypoxia and acidosis, together with hyperthermia induced by the prolonged fits.

Status epilepticus needs urgent admission; diazepam should be given at once along with 100% oxygen. It is a council of perfection to give IV drugs, but for a lone doctor with a restless patient this may be impossible, so give the first dose of 10 mg intramuscularly. If this is ineffective, a further dose may be given. By this time the ambulance crew should be able to help you control the patient and obtain venous access.

Once the fits are controlled, treat any remediable causes you have found.

Hyperventilation and metabolic acidosis

Although hyperventilation is usually due to anxiety attacks, remember to consider causes of metabolic acidosis which induce a compensatory hyperventilation. These include diabetic emergencies, overdose of aspirin, ingestion of methanol or ethylene glycol, renal failure and renal tubular acidosis.

Hypothermia is often associated with myxoedema and is common in the elderly who are isolated, demented or have sustained a fall. Coma due to hyperpyrexia may be seen following ingestion of ecstasy or other similar drugs.

ENDOCRINE *(see also Metabolic and Endocrine Emergencies p.171)*

Consider diabetic emergencies: Hypoglycaemia; Diabetic ketoacidosis; Hyperosmolar non-ketotic coma; Addisonian crisis; Thyroid disease; Myxoedema coma.

NUTRITIONAL

We are fortunate not to see severe primary malnutrition in this country, but we may see relative secondary malnutrition in those unable to absorb or metabolise nutrients for some underlying medical reason. Perhaps the most common, but not usually the isolated cause of unconsciousness, is the alcohol-dependent patient.

GENERAL INFORMATION

NEOPLASTIC

The patient who has neoplastic disease may present with a sudden loss of consciousness due to haemorrhage, overwhelming infection or as part of the expected disease process. It is likely that the underlying diagnosis is known to the patient and carers and there may even be a *'Do not resuscitate'* letter in the nursing folder. Treatment must be for the underlying cause, but inappropriate and aggressive management in a terminally ill patient is not acceptable. Care here should aim at comfort and adequate analgesia. The management plan should be discussed with the patient (if appropriate), the carers and those members of the community care team who are involved. With the patient who is not terminally ill, the new event should be investigated and treated appropriately.

DRUGS

These are dealt with in the chapter on Poisoning *(p.181)*, but the initial management of the unconscious patient with suspected poisoning is to follow the ABCs of resuscitation.

CONGENITAL

This category includes the hereditary anaemias, which may cause unconsciousness if there is a sudden fall in haemoglobin, although the most common emergency is a painful sickle cell crisis. The blood vessel obstruction caused by the sludging of the more rigid sickle cells occurs most commonly in the abdomen, back or chest, but may obstruct a cerebral vessel causing cerebro-vascular accidents. The patient needs to be discussed with their heamatologists and admitted under them as soon as possible. While awaiting admission it is reasonable to give IV crystalloids, as the patient becomes dehydrated due to the kidney's loss of concentrating ability.

VASCULAR

CVA will be dealt with under Neurological Emergencies *(p.131)*

TUBERCULOSIS

We are witnessing a resurgence of tuberculosis, particularly in the HIV-positive and immigrant populations, so tubercular meningitis and abscesses should be considered under the causes of toxic shock.

Conclusion

The unconscious patient is the ultimate challenge to the physician. The mnemonic may seem contrived, but under duress, surrounded by weeping or anxious relatives or bystanders, it is useful to have an *aide memoir* upon which to fall back. It helps to review the options during your journey to the visit and prepare your questions, examination and management.

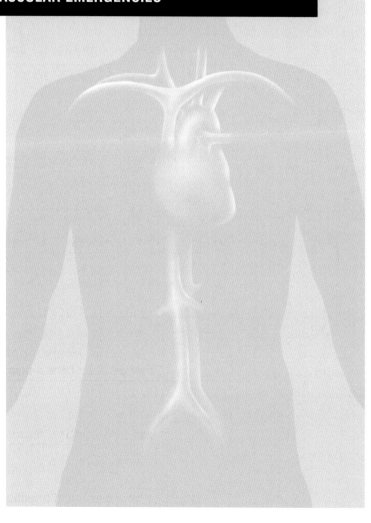

2 CARDIOVASCULAR EMERGENCIES

CARDIOVASCULAR EMERGENCIES

Myocardial infarction

Cardiac arrest

Other causes of chest pain

Acute left ventricular failure

Vascular thrombosis and arteritis

CARDIOVASCULAR EMERGENCIES

Around 60,000 people in the United Kingdom die from cardiac arrest per annum (150-200 per day) and 350,000 from ischaemic heart disease. Approximately 5% of patients who die from myocardial infarction do so in the presence of their GP. Individual Health Authorities have worked with their hospital and community services to establish integrated care pathways and public education policies, such as 'call early, call fast' for chest pain, but many patients still prefer to call their family doctor when they first feel ill.

The two key elements in the management of infarction are to save myocardium and to deal with life-threatening arrhythmias by providing a rapid response to all calls. The Department of Health has recognised this and set faster response targets for ambulance services in 1997, estimating that a further 3200 patients could be saved per annum[7]. However, some patients will have a cardiac arrest without any sign of myocardial ischaemia and they need immediate resuscitation with basic life support (BLS *see Figure Two*) before professional help arrives. Today's family doctor is required to be proficient in BLS before entering the MRCGP examination; more and more GPs are carrying defibrillators too. Basic life support will buy time, but the most common cause of cardiac

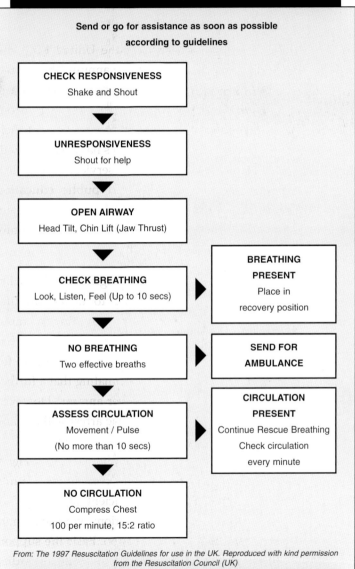

Figure Two: ADULT BASIC LIFE SUPPORT

Send or go for assistance as soon as possible according to guidelines

CHECK RESPONSIVENESS
Shake and Shout

▼

UNRESPONSIVENESS
Shout for help

▼

OPEN AIRWAY
Head Tilt, Chin Lift (Jaw Thrust)

▼

CHECK BREATHING
Look, Listen, Feel (Up to 10 secs)

▶ **BREATHING PRESENT**
Place in recovery position

▼

NO BREATHING
Two effective breaths

▶ **SEND FOR AMBULANCE**

▼

ASSESS CIRCULATION
Movement / Pulse
(No more than 10 secs)

▶ **CIRCULATION PRESENT**
Continue Rescue Breathing
Check circulation every minute

▼

NO CIRCULATION
Compress Chest
100 per minute, 15:2 ratio

From: The 1997 Resuscitation Guidelines for use in the UK. Reproduced with kind permission from the Resuscitation Council (UK)

arrest (ventricular fibrillation) only responds to defibrillation. If the first shock is delivered within eight minutes of arrest there is up to a 40% survival of hospital discharge.

MYOCARDIAL INFARCTION

History

This is the key diagnostic component of myocardial infarction since there may be no clinical signs and even ECG changes may be absent. Many infarct patients have atypical histories or are silent, so a high index of suspicion is mandatory. If the call comes to the surgery, make sure the receptionists know that all chest-pain calls should be treated as an emergency and help should be sought immediately. The practice should have a chest-pain policy. Either all patients are referred directly to the ambulance or the doctor responds at once while asking his reception staff to call an ambulance. This dual response gives the best chance of patient recovery. The ambulance personnel provide equipment and skills the doctor may not have, while the GP can respond rapidly and start to provide emergency care.

The practice policy should also include a decision about thrombolysis. In remote areas this is often provided by the family doctor, but if a rapid 'infarct to needle time' can be achieved by rapid transfer to hospital (after initial stabilisation and management), then thrombolysis need not be a GP responsibility.

Pain
Characteristically, pain is crushing, starting in the left chest, radiating down the left arm, or into the neck and around the chest; it is exacerbated by effort and sometimes relieved by glyceryl trinitrate (GTN).

Sweating
The patient feels cold and clammy and develops anxiety and light-headedness.

Other symptoms
Included here are dizziness, fluttering in the chest (from arrhythmias or palpitations), nausea, epigastric or back pain. The patient may have had intermittent angina which becomes increasingly severe - *crescendo angina*. This should be managed as an infarction and the patient admitted to hospital.

Examination
Examination may be negative, but tachycardia and hypotension may be present, as well as the classical cold, clammy skin and signs of heart failure and arrhythmias. The ECG, if you are fortunate enough to possess one, may show new changes, including elevation of the ST segment, but it may be negative. Beware of the patient with hypotension and chest-pain going through to the back. The patient may have a dissecting aortic aneurysm. Check for femoral pulses.

CARDIOVASCULAR EMERGENCIES

Initial management
After confirming the diagnosis, the patient needs strong reassurance and adequate *analgesia*. The drug of choice is diamorphine, which reduces pain, anxiety and the risk of arrhythmias (from endogenous catecholamines). Since this occasionally causes nausea, and the patient may be nauseated anyway, it can be dissolved in an antiemetic, for instance prochlorperazine. The dose of diamorphine required to relieve pain varies. Titrate it slowly IV, starting with 2.5 mg, but be aware that you may have to give up to 10 mg or more. Never give it IM as the peripheral circulation is compromised and later, when the patient's blood pressure rises, the drug may be absorbed and cause respiratory arrest. For the same reason, never give opiate analgesia unless you also carry naloxone with which to combat any respiratory compromise.

Oxygen should be given at maximum flow rates in the initial stages of management to improve the quality of the blood driven round by the remaining undamaged myocardium.

Aspirin is given early for its anti-platelet activity. *Thrombolysis* may be initiated in remote areas. In symptomatic bradycardia, vagal blockage should be induced with an initial dose of 0.5 mg atropine IV, repeated to a maximum of 3 mg until effective control is obtained.

Arrhythmias

The most common arrhythmia after an infarct is ventricular fibrillation (VF) leading to cardiac arrest (see below). Other arrhythmias are discussed under 'Other causes of chest pain' *(p.42)*. If the patient has been successfully treated for VF by defibrillation, an IV dose of lignocaine (100 mg in 10 ml as a bolus followed by an infusion of a further 100 mg in 500 ml saline) will help reduce the chance of relapsing into VF again.

CARDIAC ARREST

History

Cardiac arrests are often unwitnessed, so no history is available, and they may occur in patients with no significant medical history. The diagnosis is a clinical one, but can be supported by ECG evidence.

Examination

Assess the ABC. If the patient is unrouseable, with absent breathing and pulse, there is no need to look at the pupils or to look for cyanosis; absent breathing for 10 seconds without a palpable pulse equals cardiac arrest.

Management

Unless you have seen a current 'Do not resuscitate' order or the patient is patently unsuitable for resuscitation (traumatic injuries obviously incompatible with life, postmortem staining, monitored asystole for over 15 minutes), cardiopulmonary resuscitation (CPR) should be attempted. You are not likely to

be the only person present, so send someone to call the ambulance, giving clear instructions to state that this is a cardiac arrest. Proceed to basic life support, unless you have a defibrillator, then the first shock should be given as soon as possible. This is the shock most likely to convert the patient to sinus rhythm, but continue to administer shocks until a result or asystole is obtained. If possible, give oxygen too, by entraining it through the port of a 'Laerdal' pocket mask.

In the pregnant mother the gravid uterus obstructs the vena cava. Before commencing CPR she should be turned 15-20 degrees to her left, either by using pillows or by supporting the patient's right side upon one's knees. This shifts the uterus off the vena cava and improves cardiac output by increasing venous return to the heart (Starling's law). Alternatively, the easier but less effective manual displacement can be used.

In the European Resuscitation Council guidelines, Advanced Life Support (ALS - *see Figure Three*) follows the first three shocks, but a single GP will be fully occupied with delivering the shocks. The ambulance crew should have arrived before commencing the subsequent phases of the algorithm. Once the crew has arrived, the protocols for ALS can be initiated,

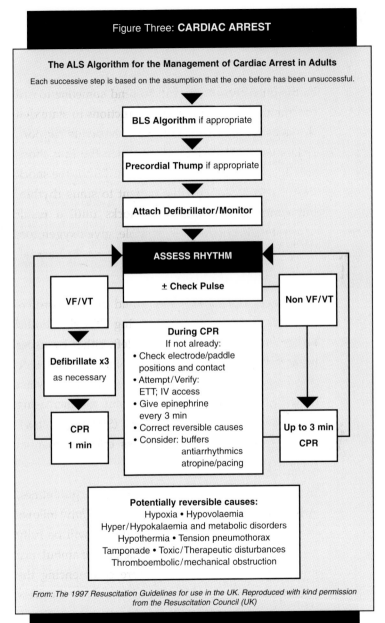

Figure Three: CARDIAC ARREST

The ALS Algorithm for the Management of Cardiac Arrest in Adults

Each successive step is based on the assumption that the one before has been unsuccessful.

▼

BLS Algorithm if appropriate

▼

Precordial Thump if appropriate

▼

Attach Defibrillator/Monitor

▼

ASSESS RHYTHM

± **Check Pulse**

VF/VT

Non VF/VT

Defibrillate x3
as necessary

During CPR
If not already:
• Check electrode/paddle
  positions and contact
• Attempt/Verify:
  ETT; IV access
• Give epinephrine
  every 3 min
• Correct reversible causes
• Consider: buffers
              antiarrhythmics
              atropine/pacing

CPR
1 min

Up to 3 min
CPR

Potentially reversible causes:
Hypoxia • Hypovolaemia
Hyper/Hypokalaemia and metabolic disorders
Hypothermia • Tension pneumothorax
Tamponade • Toxic/Therapeutic disturbances
Thromboembolic/mechanical obstruction

From: The 1997 Resuscitation Guidelines for use in the UK. Reproduced with kind permission from the Resuscitation Council (UK)

using IV adrenaline 10 ml of 1:10,000 for defibrillation persisting after the third shock and a single bolus of 3 mg atropine for asystole *(see Figure Three p.41)*.

Defibrillators
Twenty years ago the idea of having defibrillators in general practice was considered impossible, but today's defibrillator is not a cumbersome machine requiring you to read an ECG. Technology has lead to the production of semi-automatic defibrillators which analyse the rhythm for you, charges to the appropriate energy level and advises you when a shock is indicated. These machines are light, portable and self-checking. They have batteries which need no maintenance for approximately five years or 300 shocks. They can be used by all members of the practice team and are already being used by some fire brigades and police forces.

OTHER CAUSES OF CHEST PAIN

CRESCENDO ANGINA

Crescendo angina presents as angina of increasing severity and, because it implies a threatened myocardium and usually progresses to infarction, it is treated as a true infarction, even without ECG changes.

A dissecting aneurysm will present as sudden pain, often in the centre of the chest, radiating to both arm and back. It may be associated with shock and subsequent arrest. It is often diagnosed as an infarction, but a careful history, absent or asynchronous (with the radial) femoral pulses, can provide a differentiating factor. Immediate volume replacement with colloid, opiate analgesia and rapid transfer to hospital for surgery is mandatory. Complete rupture of an aneurysm will present as cardiac arrest.

PERICARDITIS

This will present as central chest pain and may radiate down the left arm. However, pericarditis is usually associated with either an existing ailment or a prodromal illness with fever and malaise. An associated effusion will cause the classic triad of signs, Beck's Triad: muffled heart sounds, raised neck veins and arterial hypotension (due to the compromised ventricles being unable to pump adequately). Again, hospital admission for drainage of the effusion and management of the underlying illness is required. Oxygen administration before admission will improve the patient's comfort.

PNEUMOTHORAX

The patient is usually in the younger age group, a SCUBA diver or a known sufferer from Chronic Obstructive Airways Disease (COAD), in whom a small pneumothorax will cause severe respiratory compromise. The patient may recall the sudden onset of pain associated with dyspnoea. The pain is related to respiration, and auscultation will reveal absent or reduced breath sounds on one side.

CARDIOVASCULAR EMERGENCIES

PLEURAL EFFUSION

This may occasionally present as an emergency, but it can be recognised by the clinical signs of reduced air entry and a dull sound upon percussion on the side of the effusion, or by symptoms of an associated disease. The trachea may be shifted away from the side of the effusion.

OSTEOCHONDRITIS

An inflammation of the costochondral junction will present as chest pain, but can be differentiated by the local tenderness and aggravation by deep breathing.

ABDOMINAL AND DIAPHRAGMATIC PATHOLOGY

This may present as chest pain, but the observant clinician will soon recognise other symptoms and signs not associated with infarction.

ARRHYTHMIAS

Arrhythmias are frequently asymptomatic, but if they lead to cardiac insufficiency and anoxia, anginal pain is felt. This may be due to supraventricular or ventricular tachycardia. The latter sometimes leads to cardiac arrest when it is managed in the same way as ventricular fibrillation, i.e. by defibrillation. Supraventricular tachycardia often responds to vasovagal manoeuvres, but if not, the patient should be admitted for treatment with adenosine in aliquots of 3 mg to a maximum of 18 mg. If this fails, then cardioversion with an initial 50 joule shock is indicated. It is unusual to attempt these latter two treatments in general practice, although some immediate care doctors with appropriate defibrillators may do so.

OTHERS

Despite a careful differential diagnosis, we can still be caught out by nerve pain (such as precedes the skin lesions of herpes zoster) or diabetic neuropathy, gastro-oesophageal and traumatic pain. When in doubt, always treat as anginal pain and refer to hospital.

Subsequent management

The patient should be transferred by ambulance to the hospital and attached to a cardiac monitor/defibrillator. The accompanying letter should include all emergency drug therapy, the time of its administration, as well as the usual patient history and examination results. Occasionally the doctor may be asked to accompany an unstable patient, but this is uncommon.

Follow-up

Patients should be encouraged to return to normal activities as soon as possible, to give up risk-inducing behaviour, as well as being aware that should there be a subsequent attack, 'call early, call fast.' Aspirin or some other medication may be prescribed. If not, the family doctor may need to prescribe something following consultation with the hospital team. Patients have the best results when they participate in an integrated post-infarction rehabilitation programme. Screening close family members may also be appropriate.

CARDIOVASCULAR EMERGENCIES

ACUTE LEFT VENTRICULAR FAILURE

Background

Left ventricular failure usually occurs to a patient in the community with known ischaemic heart disease, though it can be precipitated by low plasma proteins (due to malnutrition or hepatic disease) or fluid overload.

History

The emergency patient is likely to complain of severe dyspnoea, often of sudden onset. This frequently occurs at night. The dyspnoea of acute pulmonary oedema can be distinguished from an exacerbation of COAD by clinical examination. The past history, if available, will help differentiate between asthma or COAD and ischaemic heart disease, valvular disease or replacement valves. A review of the patient's medication will often help if a history is unavailable.

Examination

The patient in left ventricular failure has dyspnoea, ranging from mild to severe and distressing, accompanied by frothy pink sputum, intense anxiety and fear of impending death; cold, clammy skin; tachycardia; gallop rhythm and widespread crepitations. The occasional high-pitched wheeze, as heard in asthma, has led to this condition being called (erroneously) 'cardiac asthma.' The patient with COAD or acute asthma will be well-perfused and warm, with perhaps intercostal recession and tracheal tug. A single blood pressure reading is not always helpful, but should be measured to monitor progress. Failure may have been precipitated by a rise in blood pressure, which may be masked by the subsequent heart failure, and hypotension is an indication for immediate admission since the treatment of choice (frusemide) may further reduce the blood pressure.

Treatment
The treatment goals are to promote tissue oxygenation, reduce dyspnoea, and calm the patient. The treatment of choice is intravenous frusemide - initially 50 mg, but large doses (up to 250 mg) may be required. Frusemide induces pulmonary vasodilatation before the diuresis, so that symptoms will be relieved before the intense desire to pass water. Anxiety is relieved by small doses of diamorphine, again IV. The initial 2.5 mg may be dissolved in the first 50 mg of frusemide. Thereafter, the dose of both should be titrated separately. Occasionally, a slow IV injection of aminophylline 250 mg may also be needed. If control is still not obtained, a nitrate infusion may be commenced in hospital.

Subsequent management
The patient is usually admitted to hospital. If the patient is known to you, he/she can be visited again. If no deterioration occurs, then home management may be appropriate. Home care of left ventricular failure is especially effective if the failure was caused by not taking the medication in order to avoid the diuresis.

CARDIOVASCULAR EMERGENCIES

VASCULAR THROMBOSIS AND ARTERITIS

THROMBOTIC DISEASE

VENOUS

Deep venous thrombosis (DVT) is an emergency since it may lead to a pulmonary embolus. The patient frequently gives a history of leg-pain, following some form of immobility or dehydration, and has tenderness in the affected region. Anti-platelet medication may be helpful, so an immediate dose of aspirin should be given; the patient also needs to be admitted for anticoagulation. This is effective in the management of most thrombi. However, it will not benefit a pulmonary embolus once it has occurred *(see section on Pulmonary emboli p.62)*.

ARTERIAL THROMBOSIS

This is a rare but urgent emergency as it will lead to ischaemia of the area the artery serves, often a limb. The patient will have a cold, pulseless, painful limb and should be referred to the surgeons for endarterectomy or grafting.

TEMPORAL (GIANT CELL) ARTERITIS

This unpleasant autoimmune condition usually presents as a headache. A tender temporal artery may also be found. The risk of retinal artery thrombosis with subsequent loss of vision is high. An immediate dose of 40 mg prednisolone should be given, even if the disease has not been confirmed, and an urgent referral for biopsy made.

VASCULITIS

This may be in small vessels, causing a rash, or in isolated single larger vessels when it is often associated with malignancy. Treat for the underlying cause.

3 RESPIRATORY EMERGENCIES

RESPIRATORY EMERGENCIES

Asthma

Anaphylaxis

Pneumonia

Hyperventilation

Pulmonary emboli

Pneumothorax

Pleural effusion

Haemoptysis

Choking

Respiratory arrest

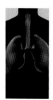

RESPIRATORY EMERGENCIES

ASTHMA

Asthma is a widespread constriction of the airways which changes in severity over time due to bronchial hyper-responsiveness. The onset may be very sudden. It is underdiagnosed and undertreated. It is responsible for around 2000 deaths per year in the United Kingdom. The severity of an attack is measured by the reduction in the predicted or normal forced expiratory volume (FEV) per second ('peak flow'). Mild asthma is a fall of FEV to 75% or more of the expected value: moderate 50-75%, severe < 50% and life-threatening < 30%. Treatment aims at reducing the bronchial smooth-muscle contraction, the mucosal oedema and inflammatory cell infiltration.

History
The severity of the attack is easily judged in the patient who is familiar with measuring his own peak flow, but other indications of severe attacks include the inability to speak in complete sentences and dyspnoea with a marked expiratory wheeze. When taking a telephone request for a visit, it is important to ask the patient to inform you of any medication they have to reduce bronchospasm while you are on your way.

Upon arrival a more thorough history can be obtained. This should include:

- The length of the current episode.

- Medication taken to relieve the current attack.

- How long the patient has been subject to asthma attacks.

- What is the usual medication.

- Is there a history of any precipitating factors?
  For example: travel, infection, animal contact, pollution, drugs or food allergens (aspirin, non-steroidal anti-inflammatory drugs - NSAIDs, food colouring or nuts).

Examination

The patient with severe asthma may appear relatively comfortable due to CO_2 retention. Look for:

- Inability to complete sentences/speak.

- Dyspnoea and cough.

- Tachycardia progressing to bradycardia in the severely ill patient.

- Tachypnoea with prolonged expiration.

- Cyanosis.

- Accessory muscle use.

- Exhaustion and coma.

Always measure the peak flow. It may not be a reliable guide to severity but can be used to monitor the effectiveness of treatment. Repeat peak flow measurements every 15-30 minutes.

Diagnosis

Figure Four shows how asthma can be divided into categories of severity depending on the peak expiratory flow measurement.

Management

- Oxygen.

- Nebulised salbutamol 5 mg or terbutaline 10 mg repeated or continuously prn.

- IV bronchodilator.

- Aminophyline 250 mg over 20 minutes.

- Salbutamol or terbutaline 250 micrograms in 10 minutes.

- Steroids - prednisolone 30-60 mg orally.

- Hydrocortisone 200 mg IV.

- Nebulised Budesonide.

ACUTE SEVERE ASTHMA

Cannot complete sentences

Respiratory rate >25 breaths per minute

Pulse rate ≥110 per minute

Peak flow <50% predicted or best

LIFE-THREATENING ASTHMA

PFR <30% predicted or best

Silent chest, cyanosis, feeble respiration

Bradycardia +/- hypotension

Exhaustion, confusion or coma

Subsequent management

- Nebulise beta-agonist at least four-hourly.

- Refer to hospital.

- Monitor peak flow.

- Continue oxygen.

Follow-up

The primary difficulty in maintaining optimum control of asthma is patient compliance with medication. The issue is one for the whole practice team together with secondary services. Asthma liaison nurses, dedicated asthma clinics, clearly written instructions and diaries for adults and children, all contribute to control. An audit trail should be established so that defaulters from clinics or repeat medication requests can be identified. Patient support groups provide some social as well as remedial activities.

ANAPHYLAXIS

Background
This is a hypersensitivity reaction mediated by IgE. Similar symptoms arise with an anaphylactoid reaction where hypersensitivity is not the mechanism. Here the term anaphylaxis is used for both since the management is similar. Both may present with angio-oedema, bronchospasm and hypotension, though some patients die from irreversible asthma without these manifestations. Other symptoms and signs may include: urticaria, vomiting, diarrhoea, abdominal pain, conjunctivitis and rhinitis.

Onset may be slow, fast or biphasic. Severity varies, usually being worse during the initial attack. Second exposure to the allergen - such as in penicillin or radiological contrast media sensitivity - causes little problem. However some allergens, such as peanuts, leave the patient with a continuing predisposition to anaphylaxis.

The wide range of symptoms and high incidence of panic attacks in patients who have had previous reactions can make the diagnosis difficult. The patient who faints after an injection may also pose a diagnostic challenge. The true anaphylactic reaction can be excluded if there are no symptoms of rash, breathing difficulty (as opposed to hyperventilation) or swelling.

Management
Adrenaline is the main treatment, but it may be associated with death from cardiac arrhythmia when given intravenously. It works best early in an attack, acting on ß-receptors, dilating

the airways, improving the force of the myocardial contraction, suppressing histamine production and enhancing its alpha-agonist effect in reducing vasodilatation. Steroids have a slow onset, so are less useful in an acute emergency. Antihistamines (H1 blockers) contribute to management, though would rarely be effective alone.

A patient undergoing an anaphylactic reaction needs to be transferred to hospital as soon as possible. Before transfer:

- Administer 0.5 ml 1:1000 adrenaline intramuscularly and repeat every five minutes until the symptoms improve.

- Give 100% oxygen.

- Consider giving 100 mg IV hydrocortisone when you have established IV access.

- Chlorpheniramine 10 mg IV.

Subsequent actions
Explain to the patient that he/she is unlikely to have a second attack unless this is a peanut or tree nut allergy, whereby patients may benefit from having a self-medication pen with adrenaline. The key to management is allergen avoidance.

PNEUMONIA

Background
Pneumonia can present as a vague malaise through to a profoundly ill patient; from classical pneumonia with sepsis, fever, pleuritic chest pain and purulent sputum, to the mildly confused or febrile older patient where pneumonitic infection is only found on routine examination. The key issues are to decide the severity of the illness and the appropriate therapy.

History
In a previously healthy young patient the presentation is usually classical - sepsis, malaise, fever, cough and chest pain. Older patients may have less focal symptoms, with the malaise and perhaps confusion as the presenting symptoms. Both groups have a fairly rapid onset. Less severe symptoms are seen in 'atypical' pneumonia. Enquire into previous attacks and those pre-existing conditions which predispose the patient to infection, such as pre-exisiting lung disease, immuno-compromised or suppressed patients, and those who are post-anaesthetic.

Examination
Fever and tachycardia are common, as is a productive cough with purulent sputum. Signs of lobar or bronchopneumonia and pleural rub may be found in the chest.

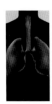

RESPIRATORY EMERGENCIES

Management

In the less severely ill there is time for an x-ray and sputum culture. Remember that the x-ray of atypical pneumonia looks much worse than the patient's symptoms suggest. If using antibiotics 'blind', then the usual treatment is:

ATYPICAL PNEUMONIA

Atypical pneumonia - erythromycin (which treats mycoplasma, chlamydia and legionella) 250 mg six-hourly for at least seven days, unless gastro-intestinal disturbance makes this impossible - then IV. Erythromycin is an irritant so avoid if patient can take oral preparation.

ACUTE LOBAR PNEUMONIA

Acute lobar pneumonia - (usually due to pneumo-coccus) amoxycillin 500 mg every eight hours IV or oral.

COAD

COAD - (likely to be infected with pneumococcus, klebsiella or gram-negative organisms) may need admission for IV antibiotics (amoxycillin plus metronida-zole and gentamycin) as well as for respiratory support.

OVERWHELMING INFECTION

Overwhelming infection - admission. When the organism has yet to be identified, IV cefotaxime plus erythromycin and gentamycin is used.

Aspirational pneumonia - (in those just discharged after day surgery or other procedures which require anaesthetic) is likely to be due to a wide range of gram-positive and negative organisms. A broad spectrum antibiotic is required, the type dependent on the severity.

Subsequent actions
Search for coexisting pathology. Correct any underlying anaemia and ameliorate chronic conditions. Consider influenza and pneumococcal vaccine for patients with COAD. General dietary and health advice is recommended, including quitting smoking.

HYPERVENTILATION

Background
Although the distress of hyperventilation is usually due to anxiety and panic attacks, remember to consider causes of metabolic acidosis *(see section on The unconscious patient p.29)* which induce compensatory hyperventilation.

History
If the initial contact is by telephone, a firm but reassuring approach needs to be taken to draw out the key features that will differentiate the organic from the psychological components. A history of diabetes or of a threatened suicide attempt, even a note, will make the diagnosis of an organic cause more likely. However, the absence of these, without a clear history of panic and the observed onset of hyperventilation in a period of distress, would indicate the need for a visit.

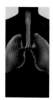

RESPIRATORY EMERGENCIES

If the caller is sensible, he/she can be instructed to breathe into a bag then call back. If this relieves the symptoms, supportive care from friends, the primary health-care team or yourself should be given, though not as an emergency call.

PULMONARY EMBOLI

History

The patient will present with sudden chest pain or collapse. There is often history of bedrest, long air travel, previous DVT, malignancy, heavy smoking or the oral contraceptive pill. The current event may be preceded by leg discomfort and ankle-swelling from deep vein thrombosis.

Examination

The patient is dyspnoeic, hypotensive and exhibiting tachycardia with pleuritic chest pain. A pleural rub may be heard on examination.

Management

This calls for urgent admission. Reassurance, oxygen administration on the journey, and good ITU care still leaves the current death rate at around 30%, and contributes to 20% hospital deaths[8]. Once the thrombus has reached the lung, anticoagulants are ineffective, though some centres try thrombolysis.

PNEUMOTHORAX

History

The patient is most likely to be a tall, thin, young male (or even a patient with Marfan's syndrome) who recalls the sudden onset of pain associated with dyspnoea. He may be a SCUBA diver or a known sufferer from COAD in whom a small pneumothorax will cause severe respiratory compromise. Progressive dyspnoea suggests a tension pneumothorax.

Examination

A simple case may have the classic signs of hyper-resonance and perhaps a raised respiratory rate, but a marked shift with progressive dyspnoea, tachycardia, engorged neck veins and hypotension with a silent chest, suggest a life-threatening tension pneumothorax. Between these two is a range of presentations which should be referred to hospital.

Management

At the severe end of the spectrum, a 14-gauge needle inserted into the second intercostal space in the mid-clavicular line on the side of the lesion will convert a tension pneumothorax into a simple one and buy time for transport to hospital.

Do not give inhaled analgesia, since the nitrous oxide diffuses into the pleural space, aggravating (or converting the simple pneumothorax into) a tension pneumothorax; oxygen does not, and should be given via a face mask. Small simple pneumothoraces are treated conservatively if there is no significant dyspnoea. Otherwise, the patient should be decompressed through a chest drain and admitted to hospital for 24 hours.

RESPIRATORY EMERGENCIES

PLEURAL EFFUSION

This may occasionally present as an emergency. It can be recognised by the clinical signs of reduced air entry and dullness to percussion on the side of the effusion. Massive effusions giving rise to respiratory distress are usually secondary to malignancy (pleural or bronchial), but also consider cardiac failure, infection and hypoproteinaemia. The latter three should be managed by treating the underlying cause. Aspiration gives relief in malignancy, despite depleting the body of essential protein. This is an in-hospital procedure.

HAEMOPTYSIS

This is possibly caused by an underlying malignancy, bleeding diatheses, tuberculosis or congenital malformations, if considerable. Minor bleeds can also result from upper respiratory tract infection. Confirm that the bleeding is a true haemoptysis and not haematemesis *(see Gastrointestinal Emergencies p.95)* and admit for management unless the volume is small and the cause known.

CHOKING*

The most common cause of choking in adults is obstruction of the glottis by a piece of food, usually something solid such as a piece of meat. The event is more common in the mentally frail adult or those under the influence of alcohol who have tried to talk, breath and eat simultaneously. Complete airway obstruction leads to collapse due to anoxia, followed shortly by cardiac arrest. Partial obstructions may be converted to complete obstruction through swelling of the larynx or manoeuvres to manipulate the obstruction.

History
The incident usually occurs whilst eating a meal. The patient grabs his throat and is unable to talk or breathe. Be aware of the polite guest holding his throat, who leaves the room silently but quickly; he may go on to an anoxic collapse in the privacy of the bathroom. This type of choking leads to the inaccurate synonym '*café coronary*'.

Examination
Early in the event (within one or two minutes) patients will be unable to speak, be holding their throat and have staring panic-stricken eyes. They will be making respiratory effort, but not moving air in or out. Subsequently they will collapse, cyanosed, first with absent breathing, then with absent circulation.

Management
If the patient is capable of co-operating, get their confidence and ask them to make one final effort to cough while you squeeze them around the chest. If this is not successful, get them to lean over a chair, with the chair-back pressing against the epigastrium, and deliver five firm blows to the parasternal muscles, adjacent to the side of T5-7. This often generates sufficient movement in the residual column of air in the lungs to shift the foreign body, so a subsequent finger sweep can

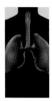

dislodge it. If this fails, move behind the patient, put your arms around him/her to meet just below the xiphisternum, lock them firmly and jerk them upwards, aiming towards the cervical spine. This forces the diaphragm upwards and causes a sharp rise in intrathoracic pressure.

If the patient is now unconscious, a similar manoeuvre can be undertaken by turning the patient on to their back, kneeling astride them and again placing locked hands in the epigastrium pushing upwards. If the patient is unconscious, attempt exhaled air resuscitation since the relaxation of the muscles with the loss of consciousness may be sufficient to allow air to pass around the obstruction. It may even allow the obstructing matter to move down to one bronchus. If this does not permit air entry, continue to alternate five thrusts with five back blows for a couple of minutes, checking the mouth for the dislodged foreign body after each cycle.

If there is no success, an emergency surgical airway should be created at the cricothyroid membrane. A sharp blade inserted into this relatively avascular area, in the mid-line between the thyroid and hyoid cartilage, will bring instant relief. It is unlikely the GP will carry surgical airways, but a series of wide-bore cannulae would serve the same purpose, though the airflow would not be optimal.

* **Choking in children is dealt with in**
  Emergencies in Children (p.190)

RESPIRATORY ARREST

The terminal event in airway obstruction is respiratory arrest, which rapidly leads to an anoxic cardiac arrest. This type of arrest has a very poor outcome (2-5% survival to hospital) but immediate CPR *(see Cardiac arrest p.39)* may buy time until advanced life support can be instituted. Alternatively, the arrest may be due to drug overdose - either by the patient himself or iatrogenic in origin. In suspected opioid overdose the antagonist naloxone is given intravenously in aliquots of 0.4 mg every two minutes. This drug works within two minutes, but has a short half-life and must be repeated to maintain efficacy. If no response is obtained after giving 10 mg, then opiates are ruled out. Flumazenil is an effective benzodiazepine antagonist, but since it works by competing for receptor sites, it itself can promote respiratory depression. Patients given antagonists need careful monitoring.

Many doctors feel it is inappropriate to carry unfamiliar drugs that are used so infrequently. Respiratory arrest can be treated with exhaled air, resuscitation, bag valve mask and oxygen. However, if a doctor is going to carry opiates for the relief of stress and pain, he would be negligent not to carry naloxone.

4 ENT EMERGENCIES

ENT EMERGENCIES

The ear

The nose

The throat

ENT EMERGENCIES

These include some of the most common dieases seen in a practice, ranging from simple coryza to severe ear infections with osteomyelitis. The former rarely cause emergency calls (except in small babies who are obligatory nose-breathers so become easily distressed). However, between these two extremes there are a range of conditions that may lead to out-of-hours calls.

Diagnosis is usually straightforward, but the emergency bag needs to be equipped with suitable diagnostic aids, including: an otoscope, plus some disposable ear pieces and spare batteries; a tuning fork (not as low a frequency as the larger ones used for testing proprioception); nasal/aural forceps; and tongue depressors. Nasal speculae and a small torch are useful for looking for foreign bodies in the nose and assessing the turbinates. The most common presenting symptoms are: pain, in the ear neck or throat; vertigo; sudden deafness; fever and malaise.

THE EAR

History

Emergencies associated with the ear usually present with ear pain. The history is directed at discovering the cause of the pain. The predominant cause is acute ear infections - *otitis media* and *otitis externa*. The ear is also the site of referred pain from the temperomandibular joint, neck muscles or cervical spine, teeth, tongue, tonsils, and larynx. The pain that precedes a visible *herpetic lesion* may also cause pain in the ear. Remember to ask about diving or travel since *barotrauma* also presents with pain. An associated URTI may suggest *otitis media*, as may measles infection, whereas preceding itching and previous attacks suggest *otitis externa*. Confirm the presence of discharge from the ear and its onset; if sudden, it is often associated with a reduction in pain as the drum perforates.

A serosanguinous discharge may mean a base of skull fracture, so enquire about recent *head trauma*. Occasionally a foreign body in the ear may present as deafness, but if it has been there for a while, it is more likely to present as an offensive discharge. *Erysipelas* is common around the ear due to haemolytic strep entering a skin break, as noted in *otitis externa*. The patient can usually describe a well-defined red area with spreading raised edge. This is associated with malaise and fever. If a *haematoma* of the pinna (following trauma) is not treated promptly, perichondritis may follow, usually due to pseudomonas pyocyanea infection. Subsequently the cartilage may collapse, giving rise to the so-called 'cauliflower' ear.

Acute hearing loss alerts us to *meningitis* and *mumps* in a younger patient, but in older patients, it is usually due to cerebrovascular events. Facial weakness may also be present. Loss is usually of more gradual onset in *acoustic neuroma* and *Ménière's* disease. Vertigo is usually due to disorders of the labyrinth and may occur suddenly in viral infection (where the

differential diagnosis must exclude hypoglycaemia, postural hypotension, aspirin overdose, cerebral ischaemia and hyperventilation). *Ménière's* disease presents as sudden severe rotational vertigo with sensorineural hearing loss and nausea and/or vomiting.

Examination

Simple diagnostic aids will clarify the underlying cause of symptoms in most cases. Examination of the ear will confirm disease of the pinna (metal or ear drop allergy, haematoma, perichondritis or erysipelas) while *otitis externa* will present as an eczematous soggy area in (and sometimes around) the external auditory meatus (EAM). A scratch to the EAM may lead to either a boil or *otitis externa*. However, the practitioner should be aware of the severe malignant *otitis externa* often seen in diabetic patients, where the infection erodes into the deeper structures involving the brain and great vessels. *Foreign bodies* usually induce *otitis externa* if left *in situ*, but early on these will be seen through the otoscope.

The patient who has an acute *otitis media* is usually in great pain and resents examination. The red/blue drum, bulging or perforated with seropurulent discharge, will confirm the diagnosis. *Barotrauma* ranges from a mildly red drum to bloody blisters on the drum, or perforation with severe vertigo. *Barotrauma* may be confused with infection if an adequate history is not obtained.

Facial weakness may be present. Skin lesions will be visible if the cause is *herpes zoster*, which affects the gasserian ganglion of the fifth cranial nerve or the geniculate ganglion of the seventh. If the fifth nerve is affected, it rarely attacks all three divisions - usually only one, with the ophthalmic being the most common. *Herpes zoster* of the seventh nerve leads to *'Ramsay Hunt Syndrome'*, characterised by deafness, periauricular lesions and facial weakness. This facial palsy does not heal as often as true *Bell's palsy*. The patient may initially present with pain, only later developing the characteristic lesions.

Patients with *vertigo* may demonstrate nystagmus. This may be continuous, especially when asked to look to the extremes of vision on either side, or it can also be induced by head movement. This might also induce vomiting and should be used only as a last resort in the diagnosis of an acutely ill patient. Nystagmus, due to labyrinthine disorders, is said to move slowly from the involved side then quickly flick back. Balance may also be unsteady and can be tested using Romberg's test. *Labyrinthitis* may not be accompanied by deafness, which is always present in *Ménière's* disease. *Tumours* and *multiple sclerosis* may also cause vertigo and should be excluded.

Management and follow-up
OTITIS MEDIA

There is great debate concerning the management of acute *otitis media* and tonsillitis. If simple analgesics and antipyretic

measures are to be used, the patient needs clear instructions as to why the regime is being suggested and how to apply it. Reviewing treatment procedures with the patient should always be arranged. If antibiotics are needed, then the most cost-effective one should be used. Resistance is rare, except in recurrent attacks, and there is no justification for the use of expensive 'kill all' medication. Your district formulary will be the best guide, but with patients who are not sensitive to penicillin, amoxycillin is well-tolerated, cost-effective and not yet resisted by too many organisms in the community. Mastoiditis is rare these days, but if it occurs (usually in immunocompromised patients), admission and surgical debridement is indicated.

OTITIS EXTERNA

Usually a home visit for *otitis externa* is not required, unless there is considerable pain. Look for an offensive odour and the spread of malignant *otitis externa*. Check the urine or blood for sugar if the patient is not a known diabetic. The organism is usually pseudomonas, often associated with a selection of anaerobes. Admission for intravenous medication is the norm. Surgical exploration may be needed to assist drainage and eradication. In less severe forms, systemic antibiotics may still be required if debris obstructs the EAM. Wicks are useful if topical therapy is used. These are inserted after aural toilet, followed by drops. Gentamycin-based drops are recommended. Wicks should be changed daily. However, persistent infection is often fungal and the ear needs thorough cleaning before applying antifungal medications.

BAROTRAUMA

Barotrauma will resolve with analgesia, if mild, but more severe cases with drum rupture need careful observation in a specialist unit in case myringoplasty is required.

ERYSIPELAS

Erysipelas responds to penicillin V, which can be given orally for seven days. If the pain is severe, 1200 units IM plus adequate analgesia accelerates recovery. Penicillin-sensitive patients respond to erythromycin. Recent *haematomata* needs drainage under local anaesthetic to prevent infection and cartilage necrosis. The risk of infection is high, so ask the patient to report any pain, fever, redness and malaise.

FOREIGN BODIES

The main danger here is not from the object itself, but from careless removal. If it does not look amenable to syringing or removal with a hook, admit for surgical removal. One attempt before admission is reasonable, unless there is obvious impaction or there are signs that it has been there some time.

HERPES ZOSTER

Treatment with antiviral drugs is rarely appropriate. Give adequate analgesia, using titrated doses, until pain is relieved.

Bell's palsy and *ophthalmic herpes* with corneal involvement needs mydriasis and topical antiviral (acyclovir) drops. Referral to a specialist unit is recommended. A patient with *Bell's palsy* is thought to recover more quickly and in a higher proportion if they receive adrenocorticotrophic hormone (ACTH) early in the disease. This, however, is hotly debated.

Otitis externa can occur with either geniculate or gasserian herpes zoster and may be the presenting complaint. A quick check for any systemic illness or malignancy should be made, but this frequently-mentioned association was found in only 1% of cases in a recent study, although 2% of patients had diabetes.

HERPES SIMPLEX

Herpes simplex needs no specific therapy, but advice about personal towels, flannels, bedding and avoiding direct contact with others is appropriate. The occasional secondary infection may need systemic antibiotics. Perioral rash may also occur in those with eczema, though the rash does not have as sudden an onset.

ACUTE VERTIGO

Acute vertigo responds to centrally-acting antiemetics, such as prochlorperazine. The patient can often be symptom-free, as long as they keep still. Acute labyrinthitis may last four to six weeks, but usually reduces in intensity over the first few days. Persistent symptoms should be investigated to exclude neoplasia.

THE NOSE

History
Nasal trauma may lead to *septal haematoma*. The GP frequently gets asked to examine a *broken nose*. If there is no septal haematoma, cosmetic intervention should be delayed, unless the injury is less than four-hours-old. Nose bleeds - due to trauma or a fragile Little's area - usually respond to simple first-aid measures, but patients are often concerned if bleeding continues.

Sinusitis - Secondary to nasal turbinates obstructing sinus drainage, this may present with pain, fever, nasal discharge, antral or frontal tenderness, along with a history of a recent cold. Any suggestion of associated orbital swelling should alert you to *orbital cellulitis*, caused by the spread of infection from the ethmoid sinuses. Children or mentally frail patients present with a nasal discharge - purulent or bloodstained - when a foreign body has been in the nose some time. Serosanguinous discharge from the nose following head trauma suggests *base of skull fracture*.

Examination
External examination will reveal most significant *traumatic injuries* with swelling and deformity, as well as the associated facial injuries. *Septal haematomata* can be seen with the aid of a nasal speculum and a good light source. Bruising around the eyes or visual disturbance should lead you to suspect associated

fractures, so refer the patient to the appropriate specialist.

Nasal discharge may be seen following head trauma with *basal skull fractures*, but is usually due to *coryza, foreign body* or *sinusitis*. Foreign bodies soon induce an offensive nasal discharge, whereas sinusitis can be identified by tenderness over the affected sinus, pain and fever. An opaque antrum can often be demonstrated in maxillary *sinusitis* when a light is inserted into the patient's mouth. Look out for *periorbital cellulitis* due to the spread into the tissues adjacent to infected ethmoid sinuses. Such infections are true emergencies, since the infection may have tracked into the brain or the cerebral portion of the meninges.

Management and follow-up
Consider immediate hospital referral for:

- Trauma.

- Difficult to remove nasal foreign bodies.

- Complex sinus infections with localised spread.

- Nose bleeds that do not respond to initial treatment.

The patient who has received a blow to the nose can be managed conservatively if there is no septal haematoma, or only a small one. A septal haematoma needs draining if it totally obstructs the nares (or it may cause septal necrosis with subsequent 'saddling' or become infected).

NOSE BLEEDS

Associated with trauma, nosebleeds usually stop with pressure if it is an isolated injury. Such nose bleeds are less easy to manage in general practice if there are other injuries. Spontaneous nose bleeds associated with a cold, in patients who have increased vascularity to Little's area, also respond to pressure for 10 minutes. However, the bleeding may persist in older patients whose vessels are less elastic. Nasal packing, left *in situ* for 12 to 24 hours will usually control this, though occasionally hospital treatment with pressure balloons or cauterising may be required.

FOREIGN BODIES

Foreign bodies recently inserted in the nose may be removed with a blunt probe while someone holds the patient (usually a child) firmly. Do not use forceps as these tend to push the offending item further into the nasal cavity.

SINUSITIS

This occurs most commonly in the maxillary sinuses. An acute attack may be aborted with steam, analgesia and local vasoconstrictive decongestants. If these treatments are ineffective, then antibiotics should be added. Long-acting tetracyclines are effective for most organisms. Chronic sinusitis may present as an emergency, though it is usually of gradual onset. It may need surgical management to improve drainage if it persists.

ENT EMERGENCIES

THE THROAT

History

TONSILLITIS

Tonsillitis usually presents as a sore throat, with dysphagia and fever due to a straightforward viral or bacterial cause, but occasionally tonsillitis is found in association with glandular fever - usually when the history is less acute. Other symptoms are often noted. Patients may tell you they can see pus on their tonsils. However, in the absence of other symptoms, it is usually the size of the swelling which concerns them, whereupon they should be reassured. Unilateral enlargement in a sick patient may be a sign of quinsy.

PHARYNGITIS AND LARYNGITIS

Pharyngitis and laryngitis will present in a similar manner and simple advice (about fluids, analgesia and temperature control by light cotton clothing or fans) rather than a visit should suffice. Always ensure the patient is happy with the advice and will call if the condition deteriorates.

Examination

It is unusual to take a head mirror on home visits, but within the surgery a head mirror and a good light will aid diagnosis. On home visits a bedside light and a tongue depressor will suffice. Fever, foetor oris and cervical adenitis all accompany tonsillitis, either with punctate pustular or diffuse lesions. Glandular fever cannot be distinguished by tonsillar examination, but by the accompanying symptoms of rash with amoxycillin, or by failure to respond to antibiotic treatment.

Occasionally a solitary apthous ulcer (periadenitis mucosa necrotica recurrens) will be found. This is similar histologically to an apthous ulcer, but single, painful and persisting for weeks. Haemorrhagic ulcers are seen in erythema multiforme and pemphigus, but the 'snail track' ulcers of pemphigus and syphilis are rare these days. A tonsillar infection with an enlarged, tender swelling on one side, often with a visible swelling, suggests a quinsy.

Treatment
The mainstay of sore throat management should be analgesia, fluids and strategies to lower the fever. Antibiotics, either immediately or in three days if there is no improvement, show little benefit[9]. An obvious quinsy should be referred for drainage, but early swelling may respond to antibiotic therapy - preferably parenteral penicillin.

5 OPHTHALMIC EMERGENCIES

OPHTHALMIC EMERGENCIES

OPHTHALMIC EMERGENCIES

EYE TRAUMA

Background

The blink reflex protects the eye from direct trauma on many occasions, but fast-flying foreign bodies, such as chips of metal when drilling, may enter the eye without leaving an obvious corneal injury or stain. A blow in the eye from an object larger than the eye socket may lead to raised pressure in the socket and a 'blow out' fracture of the orbital floor - the weakest part of the bone surrounding the eye. Do not forget to enquire about contact-lens use and remove them as soon as possible.

History

Obtain a clear description of the mechanism of injury. A report of feeling something enter the eye may not mean it is still there. The resultant abrasion may still feel like a foreign body. Ask about chemical contamination, and if this has occurred, suggest holding the head under a cool running tap with the affected eye downwards until you arrive.

If the patient has been either welding without goggles or looking at bright mountain snow for some time, ask about flashing lights or floaters, visual loss and visible discoloration. The patient may be suffering from 'arc eye', or 'snow blindness'.

Examination

Look for obvious injury to the surrounding structures as well as to the eye itself. Wash the contaminant out with copious amounts of warm water. Look for loss, reduction or blurring of vision, together with any field deficit. Also note unequal pupils or *hyphaema* (fluid level in the anterior chamber due to the presence of blood). Stain the cornea with flourescein (using a 'fluoret', a small, pre-prepared, impregnated piece of absorbent paper) to highlight any abrasions or entry wounds.

If you suspect an *intraocular foreign body*, you may wish to check after dilating the pupil with tropicamide. Remember to evert the upper lid - over an orange stick or similar device - to ensure the foreign body isn't hidden behind the upper lid. Then the foreign body can usually be removed with a cotton bud or fine forceps.

Management

If there is any injury other than a very minor one, refer the patient to an ophthalmic accident and emergency department. Taping the injured eye will reduce discomfort and prohibit further damage.

ACUTE RED EYE

Infection is responsible for most red eyes, with *viral* being the most common cause, although both *bacterial* and *chlamydial conjunctivitis* can occur. *Keratitis* is usually viral and leads to corneal ulcers. *Episcleritis*, with bilateral pink or red streaks to the episclera, is self-limiting. Arc eye also presents with a red eye, but can be differentiated by the history *(for Herpes zoster infection see p.75)*.

OPHTHALMIC EMERGENCIES

SUDDEN VISUAL LOSS

One of the most important emergencies to recognise is *acute glaucoma*. This may be revealed as acute red eye or sudden loss of vision, associated with headache and halos around bright lights. The eye looks infected with a blurred or 'steamy' lens. Adrenaline drops should be given at once and the patient transferred to hospital.

Visual deficits may be caused by cerebral or optic nerve involvment, intraoccular, retrolenticular, lenticular and superficial lesions. *Acute cerebral events*, infections or neurovascular emergencies, as well as functional disease, may cause total visual loss. *Optic nerve lesions, neuritis, central retinal arterial* or *vein occlusion, migraine* or *ischaemic optic neuritis* may also precipitate visual loss.

Retinal haemorrhage may lead to partial or complete loss of vision in a single eye, as will a *retinal detachment* or *intraocular foreign body*. Rarely, a patient will be seen who has developed an *acute cataract, severe uveitis* or *ectopic lens*.

6 GASTROINTESTINAL EMERGENCIES

GASTROINTESTINAL EMERGENCIES

GASTROINTESTINAL EMERGENCIES

THE ACUTE ABDOMEN

A cute abdominal pain presents a continuing and rewarding diagnostic challenge to the busy practitioner. The aim is to determine if there is a need for admission to hospital for surgical intervention, or whether the patient can be managed at home. The differential diagnosis includes almost all the specialities in medicine and is clarified by a critical history and physical examination. If there is doubt about the diagnosis, you should have a low threshold for referral. The symptoms may differ according to age groups. In addition, they may be modified by existing pathology and medication.

History
It is useful to keep a diagnostic algorithm in your head and work your way down, excluding or enlarging the diagnostic possibilities. The sex and age of the patient will exclude or enhance the possibility of gynaecological problems as a cause. In the young, *mesenteric adenitis* is more likely than *malignancy* or *ischaemia*: the reverse is true with elderly people.

The time and type of onset may be gradual (the malaise of *appendicitis, malignancy* or *infective conditions*) or sudden (*perforation, embolism*). It could be related to a specific activity such as eating or exercise.

The practitioner should note when taking the history:

- Is the pain localised and severe?
  (Somatic pain characteristic of *peritoneal irritation*);

- Or intermittent, as found in colic?
  (*Bowel, ureter, cystic duct*)

- Is the patient restless?
  This is often due to visceral pain, whereas the
  patient with *peritonitis* keeps still.

An evolving pattern from visceral to somatic may suggest *appendicitis, bowel strangulation* or *cholecystitis*. There are characteristic radiation patterns with *pancreatitis* (the back), *cholecystitis* (shoulder tip) and *appendicitis* (central abdominal followed by right iliac fossa).

Past medical history will alert you to previous related episodes, medication, sources of referred pain and any other modifying influences. For example *sickle cell crisis* is a common cause of severe abdominal pain in the Afro-Caribbean population.

Examination
A short period of *patient observation* before examination may reveal the level of distress and degree of movement. If the pain appears disproportionate to the physical signs, remember ischaemia. On the other hand, the elderly, immunosupressed, mentally frail or malnourished may be severely ill without exhibiting many symptoms or signs.

GASTROINTESTINAL EMERGENCIES

Auscultate the abdomen before manual examination, since the latter may increase guarding. Listen for:

- Silent abdomen *(peritonitis)*

- Rubs *(organ infarction, neoplasm)*

- Bruits *(vascular anomalies or highly vascularised masses)*

- Tinkling *(above an obstruction or severe irritation in gastrointestinal infections)*

- Normal bowel sounds

Palpation should start away from the site of pain and move gently towards it; involuntary guarding and rebound tenderness to light touch is pathognomonic of peritonitis. If the patient allows, deeper palpation should follow in order to search for masses and organ enlargement. Finally, a *rectal* and *vaginal examination* may localise the site of pain, abscesses or masses. If an obvious cause has not been found, complete a *full physical examination* to look for possible sites of referred pain.

If surgical causes are not indicated, consider the more common medical conditions that may present as acute abdominal pain - *lower lobe pneumonia, cholecystitis, pyelonephritis* and *hepatitis*. Metabolic disorders, such as *Addisonian crisis, diabetic keto-acidosis, porphyria, sickle cell crisis* and *uraemia,* should also be considered.

Investigation
Bedside urinalysis and blood sugar may give clues to urinary infection, jaundice or diabetic problems (though these may coexist with other causes of pain). Additional investigations usually have to be undertaken in hospital. However, GP co-ops based in a hospital with access to facilities may consider taking a full blood count, electrolyte and urea measurements and liver function tests. A chest x-ray and ECG may help rule out chest infection and infarction (though these are predominantly clinical diagnoses), and a straight x-ray of the abdomen may show dilated bowel and fluid levels.

Management
Patients exhibiting signs of peritoneal irritation or other surgical emergencies should be admitted after an assessment of ABC has been undertaken. Adequate parenteral analgesia and appropriate fluid resuscitation should also be given - usually with a crystalloid, such as normal saline. Acute medical emergencies can often be managed at home. In a stable patient with an uncertain diagnosis, there may be an evolving pattern of illness which can be recognised.

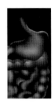

GASTROINTESTINAL EMERGENCIES

CHOLECYSTITIS

This condition responds to broad spectrum antibiotics. Tetracyclines is the treatment of choice, together with analgesia and sometimes anticholinergic anti-spasmodics, such as hyoscine 10 mg. However, this drug may cause some blurring of vision and urinary retention, so it should not be given to glaucoma patients or those with prostatic enlargement.

IRRITABLE BOWEL SYNDROME (IBS)

Severe pain in a patient with IBS can be managed at home with antispasmodics, analgesia and dietary manipulation, as well as support for any psychological problems. Occasionally, such patients develop acute diverticular disease or obstruction when admission is required.

CROHN'S DISEASE

This covers a wide spectrum of patients. Those in an acute toxic state need urgent hospital support and surgery. Milder exacerbations can be managed at home with immunosuppression, providing a close watch is kept for any deterioration of the condition.

PANCREATITIS

This is an exquisitely painful and frustrating condition for which no complete solution has been found. Patients frequently become dependent on analgesics or exacerbate their own condition with alcohol. Each case will have to be judged on its own merit. It is useful to have a patient care plan known to all members of the team, and any others likely to attend the patient, so a concerted effort can be made to control the pain effectively without inappropriate analgesia being prescribed.

GASTROINTESTINAL BLEEDING

Conveniently subdivided into upper and lower bleeds, they do not necessarily relate to the same subdivision as *haematemesis* and rectal bleeding or *melaena*. While upper GI bleeds frequently cause *heamatemesis*, they may also be responsible for *melaena* - where as little as 50 ml of blood loss per day will cause the characteristic black stool.

HAEMATEMESIS

History, examination and differential diagnosis
This can arise from:

> - *Nasal* or *pharyngeal bleeding* - the source is usually easily observed.
>
> - *Oesophageal* or *gastric tear* after prolonged vomiting (the Mallory-Weiss syndrome) can be recognised from the preceding history.   *(see over)*

(continued)

- *Peptic ulceration*, sometimes suspected on the medical history of epigastric pain related to meals, steroids or NSAID therapy, but sometimes *de novo*.

- *Oesophageal varices* - usually associated with portal hypertension and a history of alcohol abuse. Accompanied by some stigmata of liver disease - foetor oris, jaundice, spider neavae, palmar flush, liver flap, caput medusae, muscle wasting, pupura and an enlarged or shrunken liver or neoplasia.

- Occasionally a *hemoptysis* presents as haematemesis, either from swallowed blood or from the patient's misunderstanding.

MELAENA

Blood passed rectally will only present as melaena if there has been time for the blood to be altered chemically. Such blood may come from high in the GI tract or as low as the proximal colon. It may also result from swallowed blood following haemoptysis. When bleeding becomes more profuse, the blood is no longer altered. Thus, bright blood per rectum may result from an artery in the base of a *peptic ulcer*, but it is more likely to come from the lower bowel. Other possible causes include: *inflammatory bowel disease* and *antibiotic* or *radiation-induced colitis*, from *neoplasia* or *vascular abnormalities, amyloid disease, fistulae* and *haemorrhoids*.

Management
Initially this is related to palliative rather than definitive diagnosis, with the main aim being to restore circulating volume in an exanguinating patient. An ambulance should be alerted on receiving the call if there is any suggestion of major bleeding. The accident and emergency department should also be contacted once the diagnosis has been made. Colloid infusion and 100% oxygen, together with opiate analgesia, may be required. Less severe bleeds give you time to make an assessment; also consider managing the patient at home.

JAUNDICE

An emergency call pertaining to jaundices is as much related to anxiety about the patient's colour as it is to the severity of the illness. Jaundice arises from the presence of excessive bile products in the blood, either due to overproduction *(haemolysis)*, inability to metabolise (liver disease, drug-induced cholestasis) or inability to excrete (obstruction to the biliary tract). Differentiation can be obtained from history and physical examination, but definitive diagnosis requires a battery of liver function tests.

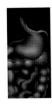

Prehepatic jaundice with *haemolysis* is a feature of the anaemias. It is less likely to need immediate admission, unless there is some form of crisis (as occurs in *leukaemia* and conditions causing massive sequestration of red cells in the spleen, such as *spherocytosis*). Then the resultant *acute anaemia* needs immediate treatment. Hepatic causes, such as *viral hepatitis*, *drug-induced jaundice* and *alcoholic hepatitis* usually respond to rest and withdrawal of any precipitating cause. Management of *secondary malignant disease* of the liver is usually conservative. These patients should be watched for any signs of deepening jaundice and drowsiness that heralds the onset of *hepatic failure*. Obstructive causes may need surgical management - *gall stones* or *malignancy of the pancreas* - while inflammatory diseases of the gallbladder respond to conservative treatment.

GASTROENTERITIS AND DIARRHOEA

Background

The causes of diarrhoea are legion, including:

- Infective organisms (bacteria, virus, parasites and fungi).

- Enterocolitis caused by antibiotics and other medication or radiation therapy.

- Inflammatory bowel disease.

- Reaction to substances found in food.

- As a response to infection elsewhere.

The diarrhoea that results from otitis media or UTIs ranks third as the cause for hospital admissions in children. The main risks are dehydration from the large amount of fluid lost through the bowel and subsequent systemic disease from toxin production.

History

Patients who have been travelling bring back a range of diseases. For example, malaria is frequently fatal and frequently missed. Therefore, it is important to ensure that you take a travel history as well as enquiring into the routine medical history. Be sure to ask about food intake, antibiotics and other medications, previous bowel diseases and other

similar cases in the house. The time of onset of the illness in relation to food intake or other patient contact, as well as the associated symptoms, are helpful in differentiating the causative agent.

Enteropathic organisms produce enterotoxins in the small bowel after colonising the mucosa. This results in profuse watery diarrhoea, which takes a day or so to take effect. This type of diarrhoea is typical in *E-coli*, *giardiasis*, *cryptosporidium* and *cholera* (at the onset) as opposed to the rapid onset of diarrhoea due to toxic substances present in food. Bloody diarrhoea is more common in cases where the organism colonises the mucosa of the large bowel (and some of the small bowel), producing ulceration such as in *shigella*, *campylobacter* and *invasive E coli*.

The principal cause of infectious travellers' diarrhoea is *E coli*, which causes a 2-3 day fulminant infection with dehydration, but rarely with vomiting. It needs differentiating from *shigellosis* or *amoebiasis*. Short, self-limiting bouts of diarrhoea without vomiting may be caused by *cryptosporidium* or *clostridia*. Other common agents, including most viral infections, induce vomiting as well as diarrhoea, but these are less virulent and usually self-limiting (2-3 day illness). The exception is a rotavirus infection, which can continue for up to two weeks.

If there is no fever and no systemic symptoms, the patient will probably recover with simple dietary advice and symptomatic treatment. This can usually be given over the telephone. Other cases probably need to be seen. Remember to consider notifying the Public Health Department if there are multiple cases.

Examination

The differential diagnosis is helped by looking for signs related to toxin production and non-gastrointestinal manifestations of the disease, as well as looking for fever and dehydration. Rotaviruses are often associated with URTI and pneumonia and are responsible for most cases of infantile gastroenteritis. Shigellosis may cause fever and fits (especially in children).Ten to twenty per cent of patients with salmonella have the classical rose spots, while others have enteric fever with meningism. Both may have relative bradycardia. Look for the enlarged liver of *amoebiasis*, although abscesses can occur elsewhere, for instance on the lung and brain.

Investigation

Stool culture should be taken before and after treatment, but if the patient fails to produce a specimen, many pathogens can be detected on a rectal swab. A full blood count is likely to help differentiate the cause by demonstrating leucocytosis (sometimes in bacterial infection), neutropenia with shift to the left (typhoid) or eosinophilia (parasites). However, blood count will not help in the initial management.

Management

This is dependent on the severity and suspected causative agent, since most patients will get better with resting the bowel and replacing lost fluids. Oral fluids should be given in

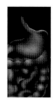

frequent small aliquots to avoid the gastrocolic reflex initiating a further bout of bowel evacuation. Prolonged dietary restriction is not recommended, since the patient needs to restore nitrogen balance to promote mucosal healing. Start with complex carbohydrates, such as rice, pasta and toast, before reintroducing the normal diet.

Most over-the-counter preparations fail to alter the course of the disease. Antibiotics should be reserved for severe toxicity in patients where the diagnosis is known or suspected. Abdominal cramps and uncontrollable diarrhoea may be helped by loperamide. If the symptoms are a manifestation of non-gastrointestinal disease, treat the underlying cause. Admission is advised for severe dehydration and persistent abdominal tenderness, particularly for the very old and the very young.

7 GENITOURINARY EMERGENCIES

GENITOURINARY EMERGENCIES

Genitourinary emergencies in the female

Emergencies around the menarche

The non-pregnant adult

The pregnant patient

Perimenopausal emergencies

Genitourinary emergencies in the male

For neonatal and childhood genitourinary emergencies see p.194

GENITOURINARY EMERGENCIES

GENITOURINARY EMERGENCIES IN THE FEMALE

Background

I t is easier to think of the 'seven ages of women' when considering this group of emergencies, since the genitourinary tract is subject to such a wide range of age- and hormone-dependent emergencies. Subdivide the patients into:

* Neonates

---

* Children

---

* Perimenarche

---

* Adult - non-pregnant

---

* Gravid

---

* Perimenopausal

---

* Postmenopausal

EMERGENCIES AROUND THE MENARCHE

UTIs continue to be a common problem. Emergencies associated with the menarche include painful and anovulatory cycles and cryptomenorrhoea, which may present as non-specific abdominal pain. Look for the bulging imperforate hymen, which can usually be cut with a sterile scalpel with little pain and considerable relief. To the patient, failure to start menstruating becomes a major emergency. Both patient and mother should be reassured that this is not indicative of congenital defects, particularly if there is a family history of late menstrual onset and the girl is clinically fit.

THE NON-PREGNANT ADULT

This group ranges from teens to menopause and is dominated by UTIs related to sexual contact. The infection may not be a classical sexually-transmitted disease, but the sexually-active woman often gets postcoital infections which culture perineal organisms, such as the E-coli group. There is a familial pattern to susceptibility to UTIs - with non-secretors of blood group antigens having a higher incidence of recurrent infection. Ascending infection leads on to pyelonephritis (reflux scarring) with fevers and malaise. Twenty per cent of women have a urinary tract infection at some time. Of those that develop reflux scarring, around 2% die. Although less likely to lead to chronic disease, careful management of these infections, with appropriate antibiotics (as indicated by culture of the urine) and follow-up until urine cultures are negative, is imperative.

GENITOURINARY EMERGENCIES

History

Patients present with dysuria, frequency and even incontinence. Patients complaining of offensive urine often feel they must have an infection, but the odour may be due to diet or medication and is an unreliable indicator. Loin pain may indicate ascending infection, but unless accompanied by tenderness in the renal angle, such pain may be due to referred pain.

Examination

This may be negative or non-specific. There usually is not a fever with cystitis, but the further the infection ascends, the higher the fever tends to be. The loins may be tender or there may be signs of pelvic inflammatory disease. Vaginal discharge, tender tubes and fornices or cervicitis may be present on vaginal examination.

Investigations and treatment

A mid-stream specimen of urine should always be taken before starting treatment. 'Multi-stix' may indicate the presence of blood, protein and nitrites. Await the results of the culture and, in milder cases, give simple advice about increasing fluids. First time cases of bacterial cystitis respond to trimethoprim. Recurrence within a month suggests a treatment failure, whereas later recurrences suggests reinfection.

Subsequent management

This group of infections may be reduced by increasing fluid intake, voiding after intercourse and discontinuing use of barrier methods of contraception. However, clusters of infections (more than three in one year) warrant investigation for an underlying disease. Precipitating causes, such as pelvic inflammatory disease and chronic cervicitis, should be eliminated.

PELVIC PAIN

Apart from urinary tract infections, the causes of pelvic pain may either be from pelvic pathology or are referred from elsewhere: the ureter or spinal cord, gall bladder, pancreas, stomach and duodenum, or even the lower lobe pneumonia. Appendicitis is the most commonly confused diagnosis. Pelvic causes include chronic pelvic inflammatory disease, endometriosis, cyclical pain, neoplasia and prolapse.

VAGINAL DISCHARGE

This is rarely an acute emergency, but is a cause of great anxiety to a patient. About ten per cent of women have excessive vaginal discharge due to cervical ectropion or adenosis, which can be treated by cautery. The more acute discharges are due to sexually-transmitted diseases and candidiasis. The former should be referred to a special treatment clinic. All the appropriate swabs must be taken before antibiotic therapy is started. Management in general practice is not easy since contact tracing is needed, but some patients refuse referral. Candida does not spontaneously occur. Look for a precipitating cause, such as drug therapy, pregnancy or diabetes if it is not sexually-transmitted.

GENITOURINARY EMERGENCIES

PELVIC INFLAMMATORY DISEASE

This is most often due to sexually-transmitted disease and is more likely in patients who are using an intra-uterine contraceptive device. It may occur after any postpartum pelvic surgery. TB should be considered in the immigrant population.

This may present as an acute emergency. Symptoms include acute loin or hypogastric pain, made worse by movement, offensive vaginal discharge and general malaise with fever. There will be lower abdominal tenderness with rebound and pain on pelvic examination, with marked cervical excitation and tenderness. If the patient allows, you may feel an inflammatory mass.

Appropriate swabs (for *anaerobes*, *chlamydia*, *gonoccocus* and basic bacterial screen) should be taken before treatment. The patient needs medication with a broad spectrum antibiotic (such as erythromycin or one of the longer-acting tetracyclines), along with metronidazole 400 mg three times a day for seven days. This course should then be repeated over the next two periods and follow-up swabs taken.

CYSTS

Ovarian cysts - These range in size from the small corpus luteum to huge cystic or malignant masses.

Cysts rarely present with pain because of the poor innervation of the ovary. Rather, they will become apparent due to complications associated with their size - pelvic impaction with urinary retention and frequency of micturition or constipation and large bowel obstruction. The treatment is dependent on the underlying effects - removal being the usual answer.

Rupture of a haemorrhagic ovarian cyst is one of the life-threatening emergencies in gynaecology, along with ruptured ectopic pregnancy and ruptured tubo-ovarian abscess. The patient is usually known to have endometriosis. The cyst may have caused pressure on adjacent organs, so that rupture has been preceded by various non-specific abdominal symptoms. When torsion and rupture occur, first there is the severe colicky hypogastric or loin pain of the torsion followed by peritoneal pain and collapse. Immediate admission is imperative, with the GP providing analgesia and fluid resuscitation.

Simple cysts also present with torsion and progressive pain due to the anoxic destruction of the cyst tissue which develop into gangrene. Other pelvic masses that may also present with torsion include pyosalpinx and pedunculated fibroid. Mittelschmerz pain is distinguished by its relationship to the menstrual cycle. It is milder and similar to the pain of haemorrhage into a corpus luteum. The latter condition either occurs in early pregnancy or occurs in a persistent corpus luteum following ovulation, which also causes delayed menstruation.

Bartholin's gland provides lubrication around the vaginal opening. Its duct frequently becomes blocked with debris leading to a cyst or even an abscess. Such abscesses become grossly enlarged and filled with pus. Initially, however, the abscess will present as a painful lump. It will usually contain mixed flora and may have *neisseria gonorrhoea* as the main pathogen. Treatment is by incision and drainage. Antibiotics have little part to play.

THE PREGNANT PATIENT

A useful dictum is to assume that, whatever the patient says, amenorrhoea preceding abnormal uterine bleeding (with or without pain) is the result of pregnancy until proved otherwise. It is not unknown for a full-term pregnancy to present as abdominal pain, with the girl denying the fact she is pregnant.

• FIRST TRIMESTER EMERGENCIES

VAGINAL BLEEDING

Unless mild and painless, vaginal bleeding usually needs referral to hospital, since many GPs prefer not to undertake vaginal examinations of the pregnant patient in an environment where there is no resuscitation facility. The alternative is to refer the patient for a scan. However, management is usually determined by the presence of an opened or closed cervical os. If open, the cervix is either incompetent or the abortion is inevitable. The patient with a closed os can be managed expectantly if a scan reveals a viable pregnancy. Profuse vagina bleeding due to the products of conception may be caused by the presence of a clot in the os, which should be removed as soon as possible.

Nonviability may be due to a blighted ovum or an ectopic pregnancy. Subsequently, the cause should be sought despite the fact that 30-40% of conceptions end in spontaneous abortion. The frequency of three consecutive abortions is only around 1%, and at this stage a referral to an early miscarriage unit is appropriate. With a closed os, bleeding may be due to a threatened abortion, when there is usually blood in the vagina, but may be caused by *vaginitis*, *cervicitis*, or *cervical neoplasm*.

ECTOPIC PREGNANCY

This usually presents with iliac fossa pain of increasing severity, which may progress to peritonism, then peritonitis. There is usually a history of a missed period and pelvic inflammatory disease or use of an intra-uterine contraceptive device. A ruptured ectopic pregnancy needs immediate admission, with fluid resuscitation, analgesia and oxygen while awaiting transport.

PELVIC PAIN

This may be due to ectopic pregnancy, infection or incarcerated uterus. The latter is unusual. It occurs in patients with a retroverted uterus or adhesions due to endometriosis. The patient starts to develop pressure on the rectum, then frequency of micturition as the pregnant uterus fails to rise out of the pelvis, getting wedged within the bony pelvis. The pain increases in severity and may be relieved by repositioning. Occasionally the visiting GP can do this by asking the patient to kneel on the bed with her buttocks in the air, while the GP

gently applies pressure from the rectum. If this is unsuccessful, the uterus needs urgent repositioning under anaesthetic.

• SECOND TRIMESTER EMERGENCIES

Although spontaneous abortion most commonly occurs in the first trimester, it can happen later. Therapeutic abortions are undertaken in this trimester for congenital defects, and anxious parents may call for advice on making a decision about an offered termination.

• THIRD TRIMESTER EMERGENCIES

VAGINAL BLEEDING

Patients with significant bleeding need immediate referral to the obstetric unit. Pelvic examination is contraindicated in the absence of full resuscitation facilities for both mother and child. *Placenta praevia* is a major cause of third trimester bleeding, and this bleeding may become catastrophic after vaginal examination. *Abruptio placenta* is due to bleeding between the uterus and separated placenta. It may seep, appearing as vaginal bleeding. However, it more usually presents as uterine or pelvic pain with later foetal distress. Neither pain nor vaginal bleeding are proportional to the size of the abruption, and any suspicion of abruption indicates a need for admission and monitoring.

Going into labour before 36 weeks gestation is the main cause of perinatal mortality. It occurs in 8-10% of all pregnancies and may be due to:

- Congenital uterine abnormalities.

- Cervical incompetence.

- Uterine infections.

- Maternal illness.

- Hormone deficiency.

- Multiple pregnancy.

- Premature placental separation.

- Hydramnios.

Again, this is beyond the scope of general practice. The patient should be referred to an obstetric unit.

PRE-ECLAMPSIA

This occurs in approximately 7% of pregnancies, more commonly in primigravidae with a family history of pre-eclamptic toxaemia (PET), diabetes, renal disease or hypertension. Patients monitored throughout pregnancy may demonstrate a gradual increase in blood pressure. Oedema and proteinuria may present suddenly with cerebral irritation or visual disturbance and abdominal pain. Pulmonary oedema may be present. The patient requires urgent admission for management. Near-term urgent stabilisation is obtained by delivering the child. In early pregnancy, attempts should be made to control blood pressure and cerebral oedema with magnesium sulphate. Antihypertensive therapy should be given intravenously. Obstetric emergencies are beyond the scope of this book.

PERIMENOPAUSAL EMERGENCIES

These are usually related to erratic and heavy vaginal bleeding. Such bleeding is caused by an imbalance of the oestrogen/progesterone hormone production. Absent menses may cause the patient to panic in case she is pregnant. Erratic menstrual cycles may be manipulated with hormone replacement therapy, but malignancy needs to be excluded. These conditions rarely present as an emergency.

___

Postmenopausal vaginal bleeding is assumed to be due to malignancy until proved otherwise. The cervix is less likely to be the cause of bleeding than the uterine body. The latter may be bulky or hard on examination, with associated bleeding from the cervical os and a pelvic mass, even a 'frozen pelvis'. Urgent, but not immediate, referral is required, unless there are signs of a urinary outflow obstruction. Then immediate admission is needed.

Like babies, postmenopausal women, particularly the elderly ones, have frail vaginal mucosa with atrophy and diminished oestrogen levels. Atrophy may be responsible for pain, dyspareunia or bleeding. Although not likely to need immediate intervention, all vaginal bleeding in elderly people should be investigated for a malignancy. Atrophy responds to topical or systemic oestrogen therapy. Occasionally very severe atrophic disease, that has advanced to vulval carcinoma, may present as an emergency. Radical surgery is usually indicated, with urgent rather than immediate referral necessary.

GENITOURINARY EMERGENCIES IN THE MALE

The male is less likely to develop urinary tract infections than the female, but if he does, an underlying anatomical abnormality as a cause should be excluded. Male genital problems relate to the penis, scrotum, testes and prostate.

117

GENITOURINARY EMERGENCIES

Emergencies associated with the penis include *balanitis* with occasional abscess formation (which are treated as other soft tissue injuries) and *paraphimosis*, which is a true emergency, needing immediate reduction of the foreskin to decrease the risk of necrosis of the glans penis. Occasionally the oedematous skin can be compressed and the foreskin returned over the glans, but if not, immediate referral for surgical incision of the foreskin under local anaesthetic is mandatory.

Testicular pain results from *orchitis, epididymitis* or *testicular* torsion; the latter being the most important to recognise since the viability of the testis is threatened if torsion is not reversed. It is most common at puberty, but may occur at any age. Torsion is often associated with the horizontal rather than vertical lie of the testis, which rotates around the spermatic cord causing ischaemia. There is sometimes a history of abdominal pain that is attributed to gastroenteritis. Pain is severe and of sudden onset if felt in the abdomen, groin or testis. Sometimes pain occurs after strenuous physical activity, but it may also occur during sleep.

Less severe pain of equally rapid onset may be due to *torsion of the appendage* testes. A blue dot may be seen on the testicular surface when it is brought near to the scrotal surface. An isolated nodule may be felt upon palpation. However, if pain precludes full examination, refer the patient to hospital to exclude the possibility of testicular torsion. If you are sure of the diagnosis, the patient can be given analgesia and managed at home. The appendage will degenerate within 10-14 days. With torsion, urgent referral with adequate analgesia is all the GP can do. Manual de-torsion should only be undertaken in hospital while awaiting surgery.

EPIDIDYMO-ORCHITIS AND ORCHITIS

Isolated orchitis is usually found in association with or as part of a wider disease, such as mumps, viral illness or syphilis. Epididymo-orchitis presents with a slower onset of pain than torsion, but may be equally painful in the final analysis. The former is found in association with urethral discharge and frequency of micturition. It has age-related causative organisms. In young boys it may indicate congenital anomalies which cause urinary stasis, so after treating the infection, further investigation is required. In adolescents and young men, it is most likely to be secondary to sexually-transmitted disease.

Older patients develop infections due to E-coli or klebsiella due to urinary outflow obstruction, usually secondary to *benign prostatic hypertrophy* (BPH). This may also cause *acute retention* and retention with overflow. Always check the bladder and refer patients to accident and emergency for first-time acute retention, although conservative measures, such as putting the patient in a warm bath and running adjacent taps, are frequently effective. Less common causes of urinary retention are *urethral stricture*, medication with sympathomimetic agents, or some underlying neurological disease.

GENITOURINARY EMERGENCIES

RENAL COLIC

Renal colic usually presents as acute abdominal pain radiating from the loin to the testis, depending on the site of the obstruction, in association with haematuria, sweating, nausea and vomiting. The most likely cause of renal colic is a stone, but extrinsic causes, such as neoplasms, may impinge on the ureter. Urological stone disease is three times more common in males and has a familial tendency. Sedentary jobs and poor fluid intake, as well as climatic conditions, influence both stone formation and the development of colic.

Patients with recurrent attacks may be managed at home while awaiting definitive surgical management, but most patients are referred to accident and emergency. Analgesia needs to be adequate, but addiction is a common problem. Hospital investigation should locate the site of the stone and any underlying renal impairment, as well as determine the need for surgical intervention to correct congenital abnormalities or remove recalcitrant larger stones. NSAIDs in adequate dosage (diclofenac sodium 75 mg IM) will be effective in many cases.

ACUTE RENAL FAILURE

Acute renal failure may present in an already sick patient, perhaps undergoing dialysis, or, more rarely, as a primary event from pre-renal, renal or post-renal causes. It may be oliguric or non-oliguric and the patient is often acidotic *(see The unconscious patient p.29)*. Confusion, hypertension, pulmonary oedema or pericarditis may be apparent. An arteriovenous fistula in the arm may be the first clue to the diagnosis of renal failure. Admission to a renal unit is required.

8 PSYCHIATRIC EMERGENCIES

CHAPTER EIGHT

PSYCHIATRIC EMERGENCIES

Admissions under the Mental Health Act 1983

PSYCHIATRIC EMERGENCIES

Background

Consultations with patients who are disturbed can be stressful and full of pitfalls. The purpose of your assessment is to get a clear understanding of the psychological or psychiatric process, so that an informed decision can be made about immediate management. Care may occasionally involve compulsory admission under the Mental Health Act 1983. Only a minority of disturbed patients are violent, but it is sensible not to examine a violent patient alone, or one with a previous history of violence.

History

The relatives of patients with psychiatric symptoms are often the best source of information, together with previous records and consultation with other members of the practice team. Many patients with such emergencies may present to the surgery. However, the more seriously disturbed do not seek help for themselves and are often incapable of giving you a useful history. If the initial contact is with a relative over the telephone, try to obtain as much information as possible from the caller, since these patients are often intolerant of relatives or carers giving their version of events.

Key features are:

- The speed of onset of the event.

- The precipitating causes, such as recreational drugs, alcohol, emotional conflicts, change or omission of medication.

- Any previous episodes and treatment.

The practitioner should also ask:

- Is the patient at risk of self-harm or a danger to those around him/her at the moment?

- What social support is available, both now and long-term?

If there is any chance that the patient is truly violent, you may have to ask the police to accompany you on the visit, though it is best if they keep a low profile until you need their support. When the consultation takes place in the surgery, keep the door open if you feel insecure and position yourself between the door and the patient. Remember to use techniques for diffusing anger rather than responding in a combative manner yourself.

PSYCHIATRIC EMERGENCIES

Examination

A full physical examination will rule out organic causes of acute psychosis (infection, hypoglycaemia, hypoxia, drugs or even delirium tremens). Perform a comprehensive mental state assessment:

- Is the patient unkempt?

- Are they orientated in time and place?

- What is their mental test and anxiety/depression rating score?

- Are they depressed in appearance or dehydrated?

- Do they have suicidal thoughts or an inability to plan ahead?

- Have they considered a method of suicide in detail?

- Are there feelings of unworthiness?

Initial management

The diagnosis should now be clear. If there is an organic cause, this may respond to treatment of the underlying disease. However, sedation may be required. The main urgent psychiatric problems can be divided into the *functional psychoses* (the most common being *manic depressive disorder* and *schizophrenia*) and *affective disorders* (*depression, anxiety, mania*). Less frequent emergencies will include *puerperal psychoses* and *drug-* and *alcohol-related problems*.

After coming to a diagnosis and deciding if the patient needs treatment, you then have to decide if this treatment can be given in the community or whether the patient needs admitting. Psychoses usually need immediate medication, whereas less severe cases of affective illness can sometimes be managed with psychological interventions based in primary care. Does the patient understand this need or do you and the relatives, together with a social worker, have to take steps to protect the patient through formal section?

Occasionally, the patient is so disturbed that a neuroleptic has to be given immediately for its initial sedative effect, which precedes the anti-psychotic one. The treatment of choice is intramuscular haloperidol (2-10 mg, increasing to 30 mg if necessary). If the patient will take oral medication, then chlorpromazine is ideal (25-100 mg); but this should not be given intramuscularly if the patient requires community care, as it can lead to severe cardiovascular collapse. For severe anxiety and agitation a benzodiazepine is effective. Remember that too small a dose may disinhibit the aggressive patient. The rate of absorption from an intramuscular injection is variable, so either rectal or intravenous administration is preferred. Because diazepam is an irritant, it is either given as an emulsion or by withdrawing blood before and flushing after administration. The dose range is wide (from 2-20 mg) since patients vary in their response.

PSYCHIATRIC EMERGENCIES

ADMISSIONS UNDER THE MENTAL HEALTH ACT 1983

If your assessment deems hospital treatment necessary and the patient refuses, a compulsory admission can be arranged under the above act. The most likely sections you will use are 4 (admission for assessment in an emergency) and 2 (admission for assessment for 28 days, usually when there is no previous history of mental disorder). Section four requires the signature of a doctor (who need not be approved under section 12 of the act) and a social worker (who should have seen the patient in the previous 24 hours) or the next of kin. This section allows the person to be held for 72 hours, providing they are admitted within 24 hours of the application being completed. Section 2 can then be completed by two doctors, one of whom is approved, and a social worker. In practice this is usually the patient's family doctor and the hospital doctor. Sometimes, during the working day, the relevant people are available to complete a section 2 admission immediately.

Other sections occasionally used in emergency situations, in which the GP may become involved, are 135 and 136. The former, which allows a social worker to apply to the magistrate in order to remove a patient to a place of safety whenever it is felt he/she is incapable of caring for him/herself, is being neglected or abused. Section 136 allows the police to remove a mentally disturbed patient to a place of safety (usually the police station or local accident and emergency department) for assessment by a doctor and approved social worker.

Subsequent management
Ensure the ambulance service is aware that the patient is being admitted under the Mental Health Act. Some services insist that a social worker or family member travels with the patient. For patients remaining at home, provide sufficient emergency medication and advice on when to contact you should the patient's condition begin to deteriorate. Clarify who is to make contact with the appropriate psychological support. Some services prefer the patient to make the contact, while others need a doctor's letter. Arrange follow-up appointments. Make a note to check that they have been in contact with suitable support groups. Families may also appreciate being put in touch with family support associations.

9 NEUROLOGICAL EMERGENCIES

CHAPTER NINE

NEUROLOGICAL EMERGENCIES

Fits

Sudden focal neurological deficit

Headache

Acute confusional states

Guillain-Barré Syndrome

Bell's Palsy

NEUROLOGICAL EMERGENCIES

FITS

Background

These range in presentation from a single febrile fit to status epilepticus. The initial management, after dealing with the ABCs of resuscitation, is to control the fit before seeking the cause. Some fits are self-limiting, but status epilepticus needs controlling, since hypoxia and acidosis will lead to permanent brain damage, as will the hyperthermia induced by the prolonged fits. A mnemonic useful for recalling the causes of fits is **'Vowels and Fits'**.

AEIOU FFIITTSS

- **A**lcohol
- **E**pilepsy
- **I**nsulin-hypoglycaemia
- **O**verdose
- **U**raemia and other metabolic causes

• **F**ever	• **F**unctional
• **I**nfection	• **I**schaemia or hypoxia
• **T**rauma	• **T**umour
• **S**troke	• **S**hock (including anaphylactic)

Note: Fits in children are dealt with on p.198

History

This is directed at finding the precipitating factors for the present fit. Also note any previous history of fits, current medication, alcohol use or consumption, the presence of diabetes, allergies or psychological disturbance.

Examination

If the patient is in the active stages of a fit, rather than postictal, it is difficult to undertake any form of examination. All you need to do then is protect the patient from hurting themselves. Once activity has settled, confirm the patient is able to breath and has a pulse, then seek the cause of the fit. If the patient is a known epileptic, there may be little to find unless some inter-current illness has interrupted the usual medication regime. Occasionally a patient may develop a focal motor lesion after a fit which outlasts the postictal phase. This is called *Todd's paralysis* and usually resolves within 24 hours.

Look for signs of any known associated causes. With a first fit in a previously healthy patient, a much greater work-up is required. Referral to hospital is appropriate, even if not immediate. Fever rarely induces fits in adults; therefore, you must check for focal neurology, infections and all the causes listed under 'Vowels and Fits'. Measure blood sugar and test urine. If the patient develops subsequent fits or goes into status epilepticus, move on to seizure management while continuing your examination during quiescent periods.

Immediate management

Diazepam should be given at once, along with 100% oxygen. If possible, give it IV. This may be impossible, so give the first dose of 10 mg intramuscularly. If this is ineffective, a further dose may be given. Although there are other drugs used to control fits in accident and emergency, the GP should stick with the one treatment with which he is most familiar, since his need for such therapy is limited. Diazepam is also the treatment of choice in *eclamptic fits*, but the ultimate treatment for eclampsia is urgent delivery of the child who is also at risk from anoxia. This risk will be compounded by respiratory depression induced by the sedation given to the mother. Contact the obstetric unit immediately. Once the fits are controlled, treat any remediable cause you have found - hypoglycaemia with 50 mg dextrose IV in 50 ml water, and anoxia by continuing to give 100% oxygen.

Subsequent management

Manage the underlying cause. Ensure therapeutic levels of medication. Remind patients of their duty to inform the DVLA, where appropriate, that they have epilepsy. If the patient is to be managed at home, ensure there is a carer around who knows how to contact you if the patient's condition deteriorates.

SUDDEN FOCAL NEUROLOGICAL DEFICIT

Introduction

Most patients presenting with a stroke have a focal neurological deficit. Such deficits may be hidden in the deeply unconscious patient. Clinically it is difficult to distinguish between thrombotic or haemorrhagic strokes, but unless they present very late with only a small deficit, they should be admitted. Stroke patients respond better in a dedicated multidisciplinary stroke unit, preferably one with an acute unit and a rehabilitation unit[10]. American doctors have shown that thrombotic strokes respond better with thrombolysis if given within three hours of onset. Unfortunately, the accuracy of diagnosis, even with computerised tomography (CT), is not good and concerns have been expressed about inducing deaths from haemorrhagic strokes.

History

This is aimed at distinguishing the patient in need of immediate resuscitation from one who can have a more measured response. An accurate history can help differentiate acute strokes from other causes of unconsciousness, while identifying those focal neurological deficits which would benefit from immediate surgical intervention. Occasionally a transient ischaemic attack can be distinguished from a permanent event, but this is usually a retrospective diagnosis. A young female patient who collapses suddenly may have a subarachnoid haemorrhage or embolism, though both can occur at any time of life. Also consider focal epilepsy or atypical migraine, and check for a history of either fits or head pain.

NEUROLOGICAL EMERGENCIES

Remember to enquire about:

- Existing cardiovascular pathology

- Hypertension

- Atrial fibrillation or subacute bacterial endocarditis (SBE)

- Past history of similar episodes

- Diabetes and other illnesses

Examination

After ensuring the ABCs are controlled, move to a rapid neurological assessment (AVPU), then GCS. Initially check for hypertension, left ventricular failure and neck stiffness. Then go on to check focal signs, including signs of small peripheral emboli (splinter haemorrhage, skin lesions) and arrythmias. Measure blood sugar, since hypoglycaemia can present as unilateral weakness.

Management

Arrange for an ambulance, if this has not already been done, and give the patient 100% oxygen. Establish an open airway, breathing and circulation, and place the patient in a comfortable position without compromising the airway. Hypertension is best managed in hospital. Lowering the BP will reduce the amount of brain damage.

Subsequent management

Liaise with the hospital and community teams. Management will be dependent on progress and outcome. Aftercare will range from full supportive care to supervision of aspirin or antihypertensive therapy and general health care, such as weight control, exercise and diet. 'Stroke clubs' have proved beneficial in rehabilitation.

HEADACHE

This is such a common symptom that we need to distinguish the serious from the trivial. A patient with a previous history of similar attacks is less worrying than one with a new and different headache of sudden onset.

Consider the following:

MENINGITIS

Bilateral pain, progressive with other signs of meningeal infection.

ACUTE NEUROLOGICAL DEFICIT

Particularly subarachnoid haemorrhage - severe sudden onset, bilateral, often occipital.

NEUROLOGICAL EMERGENCIES

RAISED INTRACRANIAL PRESSURE (ICP)

Worse in mornings and on straining.

MIGRAINE

Usually unilateral associated with prodrome, nausea and may occur in clusters or after trigger factors, such as alcohol and chocolate.

TENSION HEADACHE

Usually of more chronic onset, associated with stress.

TEMPORAL ARTERITIS

Visual loss, tender artery, subacute onset.

ENT INFECTIONS

Associated fever, tenderness or visible inflammation of the affected part.

CERVICAL SPONDYLOSIS AND NECK TRAUMA

History and cervical spine signs.

Treatment depends on the aetiology. Trigeminal neuralgia needs urgent steroids, and meningitis needs antibiotics, then admission. Any suggestion of raised ICP and deficit also requires admission.

ACUTE CONFUSIONAL STATES

These may be superimposed on an already frail mental state, for instance in elderly people, when a mild physiological insult will tip the balance. The causes are often age-related. The young are most likely to become confused following the use of recreational drugs, while those at the extremes of age are very sensitive to hypoxia, septicaemia, infections of the respiratory or urinary tract and anaemia. Carbon monoxide poisoning and other chemical insult may present as confusion. The history is best obtained from a source other than the patient. Most patients will need admission for investigation and management.

GUILLAIN-BARRÉ SYNDROME

This is a rare form of paralysis which presents as ascending paralysis due to demyelination. It may cause unconsciousness due to the anoxia induced by chest-muscle paralysis. At its onset patients are often thought to be hysterical, until it progresses. Oxygen and respiratory support is needed during transport to the hospital, where specific effective treatment (ITU support and plasmapheresis) may be given.

BELL'S PALSY

This is the most common cause of facial weakness; it may be preceded by pain around the ear without herpetic lesions. It is a true lower motor lesion of the facial nerve, causing all the muscles on the affected side to be paralysed (unlike a higher vascular lesion where the facial weakness often leaves the forehead muscles functioning due to cross innervation). Patients often think this is the start of a stroke.

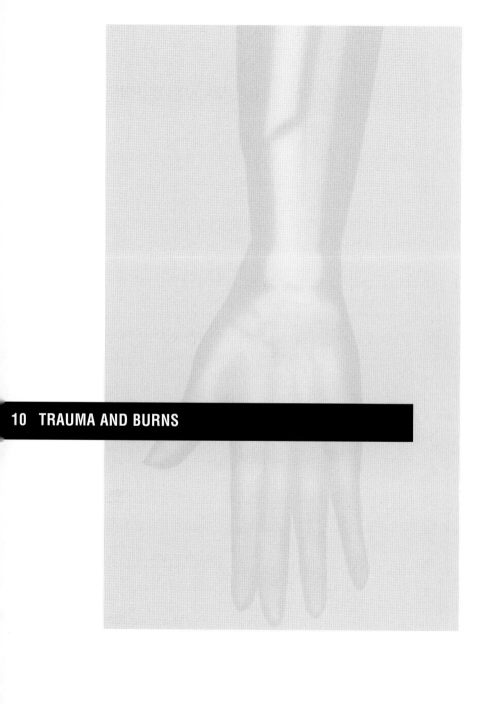

10 TRAUMA AND BURNS

TRAUMA AND BURNS

Road traffic accidents

Minor injuries

Sprains and strains

Burns and scalds

TRAUMA AND BURNS

ROAD TRAFFIC ACCIDENTS

Introduction

Many doctors feel it is not their role to attend victims of road traffic accidents, but if you are passing an accident or one occurs outside your surgery, you will have little choice. Similarly, you are likely to be called to accidents occurring in the home or on industrial premises. Road traffic accidents are the most common cause of death in patients between 1 and 15 years. Since the younger patient is probably fit before the incident, they have an excellent chance of recovery if appropriate treatment is initiated promptly.

History

If the patient is unable to give a history about the events leading to the accident, then try to get one from a bystander. In trauma, the mechanism of injury alerts you to the likely associated injuries - falls from a height on to the feet lead to calcanial fractures and associated lumbar spine injuries, whereas a head-on impact in a car is likely to cause whiplash, sternal injuries from the steering wheel and posterior dislocation of the hip, as the car engine compartment shifts back onto the knees. The severity of injury is related to the amount of restraint, speed of impact and the presence of protection - air bags, nets or structures that break a fall, and some forms of protective clothing.

Immediate-care doctors carry Polaroid cameras to photograph the accident site with the patient *in situ*; it saves a hundred words and encourages doctors in casualty to accept your story when you deliver a well-packaged and resuscitated patient!

Examination
First ensure that the scene is safe for you to approach - there is little point in you becoming a second casualty. Ask bystanders to provide protection of the accident scene (direct traffic until police arrive, keep observers away from the area etc.). Ensure an ambulance has been called and perform a competent primary survey (The ABC), then disability (D) with AVPU while awaiting its arrival. Only after assessing and controlling these do you proceed to the full secondary survey from top to toe. Again, in the home a similar assessment should be made by the visiting doctor. All accident sites are considered 'scenes of crime' so do not disturb the area needlessly, although a thorough examination must be made.

Management
The airway may need to be maintained with chin support and jaw thrust. In a road accident, often a passer-by will help with this while you continue your assessment. In a factory, this should be carried out by the recognised first-aider. If there is any chance of cervical spine injury, ensure the neck is kept in line and not over-zealously tilted, converting an unstable fracture into a spinal cord injury. In a multiple casualty incident, unless there are several skilled assistants, the patient

in whom you detect no respiratory effort should be presumed dead while you assess other victims for circulation.

In a single patient incident, mouth-to-mouth exhaled air ventilation, using a pocket mask with entrained oxygen, is effective if you are not used to other airway techniques. One classic fracture seen at the roadside that needs immediate treatment is *Le Fort type three fracture*, which allows the middle third of the face to move backwards, potentially obstructing the airway (stove-in face or dish face). Here the patient will have received a direct blow, causing a fracture across the face through the floor of the orbit and separating the zygomatic arches. If you put your fingers into the mouth and hook them behind the soft palate, the whole section will move forward (albeit with a sickening crunch). The restored patent airway should be maintained with some form of airway device, preferably an endotracheal tube.

All trauma victims benefit from oxygen at high flow. Patients who are trapped are best left *in situ*, unless there are greater risks remaining in the vehicle, for instance instability on a cliffside or fire. Those that are not trapped and are conscious may have already left the immediate accident site, so try to restrain them as walking wounded may still have severe injuries, as well as being required to give evidence to the authorities.

Bleeding should be controlled with firm pressure and elevation if in a limb. If the unconsciousness is thought to be secondary to haemorrhage, a large venous cannula should be inserted and 500 ml colloid given as fast as possible. There is great debate as to whether IV fluids aggravate traumatic injuries by keeping the blood pressure artificially high, thereby encouraging bleeding, but there is no argument about their use in massive haemorrhage where two cannulae are used routinely. It is unlikely that you will have time to set up two drips before the paramedic arrives to help you. Aim to keep the systolic blood pressure above 90 mm/Hg.

With head-injured patients, expedite admission, give oxygen and control bleeding. Morbidity and mortality are directly proportional to the delay from the incident to theatre time, with secondary brain damage occurring due to anoxia.

Pain, particularly that due to fractures, is helped by reassurance, positioning and traction, as well as analgesia. If analgesia is to be given, it should be adequate, intravenous (unless you carry oxygen/nitrous oxide mixtures) and recorded. Intramuscular drugs are poorly absorbed due to peripheral vascular shut-down and then later - when the patient is recovering his/her peripheral perfusion - they can receive an inappropriate analgesic boost that may cause respiratory depression or arrest. Opiates are most suitable, and the powder form of diamorphine is soluble in most antiemetics. They should be given simultaneously. In the head-injured patient be cautious

with analgesia, but if the Glasgow trauma score remains steady, small aliquots may be given.

When the ambulance arrives, it helps if you give the paramedic a quick resumé. After deciding if they need to send for additional support, ask the crew to see the patients who are most severely injured, and offer to travel with the injured in the ambulance.

Subsequent action
Remember to keep contemporaneous notes as you may have to make a statement or appear in court later, where only notes made at the time are acceptable. Fortunately, dictated notes are admissable, so keep your pocket dictating machine in the car for such eventualities.

MINOR INJURIES

This area of emergency medicine does not seem to have been dealt with well by family doctors. It was considered unimportant during our education compared with the more serious injuries. Lack of confidence, combined with an over-optimistic faith in x-rays, results in GPs referring such patients to hospital for management (if the patient had not already attended accident and emergency himself).

Nurse practitioner-led Minor Injuries Units are being established either alongside, or are replacing, existing accident and emergency departments. These work closely with, or employ, local GPs. Nurses routinely deal with minor lacerations, peripheral limb injuries, foreign bodies, boils and grazes, and can order and interpret a limited range of x-rays.

Well-managed minor injuries give great job satisfaction, but poorly managed ones can lead to major complications. In any minor injury with a break in the skin, always consider tetanus status. Ensure there is no neurovascular compromise or damage to underlying structures, nor any residual foreign body or a possible associated fracture.

WOUNDS

Incised wounds are usually clean, bleed profusely and rarely get infected. They should be sutured, if good apposition cannot be obtained, with dressings or glue. Problems arise when there is damage to underlying structures, such as tendons, nerves and vessels, or if the incision is over a joint. In these cases, referral to accident and emergency is appropriate.

Penetrating wounds may appear minor superficially. However, their depth is often unknown. Size may be gauged by the size of the implement used, if it is available, but referral to accident and emergency is usual. Stab wounds involving deep structures may require fluid resuscitation before or during transfer.

Abrasions range from a small superficial graze to a large friction burn from clothing, classically in a motorcycle accident. They are often very painful and can become infected.

Fingernail scratches and evidence of assault need careful recording as they may be called as evidence later.

Gunshot wounds are becoming increasingly common, but accidental and deliberate shooting may be reduced by our new gun laws. Injury is dependent on the type of weapon, the speed of the bullet(s), the distance of the gun from the patient and the site of injury. All will require hospital investigation. Initial management should involve a careful recording of the circumstances. You may be required to resuscitate, dress wounds and administer analgesics where appropriate.

Hydraulic injuries are commonly found in those people who use high-pressure injection techniques for industry or home-car maintenance. Air or chemicals enter through an apparently minor wound, where the tissues are forced apart, and later there may be necrosis. These wounds are particularly painful on the fingers. All need referral.

Dermatitis artifacta or **putative injuries** can be suspected when bizarre-shaped wounds, usually caused by less painful mechanisms (sharp instruments), are found on easily accessible sites.

Foreign bodies - These may complicate penetrating wounds and be in any body cavity. If the history is clear, the foreign body (FB) is visible and if you feel confident that you can remove it with the means at your disposal, there is no need for referral. If the FB has been present some time, there is a chance it has fragmented. If the patient is unsure of the type or place of entry, refer to the hospital.

Animal bites - These often introduce virulent organisms deep into the soft tissues, and since *clostridia* is often present in the mouths of cats and humans, gas gangrene may develop.

Human bites - The patient with an apparently minor injury on the knuckles from punching someone in the mouth may later develop deep soft-tissue infection, tracking the hand and forearm. Such lesions often present late, since the perpetrator is both ashamed, under the influence of alcohol and unaware the wound was serious. Human bites are common in fights and in prisoners attempting to escape human forms of restraint. The local injury needs cleaning, as well as tetanus and antibiotic cover (metronidazole 400 mg tds for 10 days with augmentin or erythromycin for five days). The patient also needs screening for any transmitted disease - hepatitis B or C or HIV.

Cat and dog bites are relatively innocuous compared with human bites, though the latter, when given by a large dog, can cause considerable soft-tissue and bony damage. Patients who are bitten by rabid dogs may need both prophylactic antibiotics and antirabies serum. The latter medication is held by public health laboratories, who will provide it (and good

TRAUMA AND BURNS

advice) promptly. It should be given in a divided first dose - half adjacent to the wound, the other portion intramuscularly, preferably in the arm. Initially it needs giving daily, then in decreasing frequency over three months.

SPRAINS AND STRAINS

Introduction

The busy GP needs some rules of thumb concerning the need for referral, particularly for radiographic diagnostic support and various protocols that have been devised which differentiate the areas of concern. One excellent group of protocols are the 'Ottawa Rules' *(see Figure Five)*. Those for ankle injury give a 97% accuracy and stipulate the only conditions under which you need to x-ray either the ankle or foot[11].

History

As with most accidents, the mechanism of injury gives a strong clue to its extent of resultant damage. The time since the injury and the appearance of swelling are also very useful indicators. For example, a knee with immediate swelling suggests an *haemarthrosis*, whereas more gradual onset of an effusion suggests fluid. The level of pain can be misleading, as can the level of disability, but together with other clues - referred pain, discoloration

OTTOWA ANKLE RULES

Ankles need an x-ray series if there is any pain in the malleolar zone and any of these findings:

☐ Bone tenderness at posterior edge
  or tip of lateral malleolus.

☐ Bone tenderness over
  medial malleolus.

☐ Inability to bear weight both immediately
  and when seen at surgery.

A foot x-ray series is only required when there is any pain in the mid-foot zone and any of these findings:

☐ Bone tenderness at the base of
  the fifth metatarsal.

☐ Bone tenderness
  over the navicular.

☐ Inability to bear weight both immediately
  and when seen at surgery.

Similar Ottawa Rules have been devised for other areas.

and deformity - a picture soon appears. Remember to enquire about other conditions - anticoagulant therapy, bleeding diatheses and general health.

Examination
Providing the environment is safe, examine the patient where you find them. Look for swelling and tenderness, asymmetry, deformity, loss of function and (usually when applying support such as a splint) crepitus or abnormal movement.

Management
The triad of **Ice, Compression** and **Elevation** (ICE) comforts and promotes healing in most sprains and strains. However, if there is any suspicion of a fracture, refer to the hospital. Knee injuries present a diagnostic challenge. For example, a painful knee with additional movements (excess lateral or medial movement) may have medial or lateral ligament disruption. Torn cruciate ligament would exhibit excessive forward or backward knee movement, while reduced movement and locking may indicate cartilage tears or loose bodies in the joint. It is usual for orthopaedic surgeons to deal with these injuries immediately, performing arthroscopies to confirm the exact damage. This is particularly important in professional sportsmen who wish to rehabilitate and function normally as soon as possible.

BURNS AND SCALDS

Basic management principles

Whatever the type of burn - scald, thermal, chemical, radiation or electrical - there are basic management principles. The *first* is to protect yourself from becoming a casualty. The *second* is to reduce the damage being caused at the time of the incident by removing the patient from the source and neutralising it if appropriate. Cool thermal burns and scalds with copious amounts of running water. Dilute chemical burns (with the exception of substances such as crystalline lime, which generate heat on contact with water or phosphorus which explodes) and turn off the power source with electrical burns. *Thirdly* proceed to assessment and the ABCD.

THE AIRWAY

The airway may seem to be intact with a normal respiratory rate. After fires in a closed space or with explosions, look carefully for singed nasal hair, carboniferous material in the nose, mouth or further down the airway. Look for redness and soreness, suggesting inhaled hot air and perioral or perinasal burns. Such patients may rapidly develop oedema and airway obstruction and should therefore be given 100% oxygen and transferred to hospital by a paramedic ambulance, with the knowledge that an endotracheal tube will need inserting in the unconscious patient, either selectively on site or during transport if the patient deteriorates.

Fires also generate toxic fumes and carbon monoxide, including cyanide, which should be assumed in a patient with high carbon monoxide levels. The cherry-red coloration of erythrocytes noted when fixed in burned tissue is not as obvious as textbooks lead us to believe, unless the patient is moribund. Other indications of cyanide include dilated pupils, metabolic acidosis and myocardial depression.

BREATHING

Breathing may be impaired through direct lung damage, shock or toxins. One hundred per cent oxygen should be given, as well as ventilatory support through exhaled air resuscitation or bag valve mask. Breathing will also be impaired if the chest is splinted by circumferential full-thickness burns, which become completely rigid. These must be cut at various sites - from top to bottom and all round - from where it bleeds to where it bleeds (which sadly is also from where it hurts to where it hurts). Such incisions are called escharotomies and require strong scissors (as well as a strong stomach!). If there are chest burns to this extent, the patient may well be unconscious but if not, opiate analgesia is required.

CIRCULATION

Circulation may be impaired, both through fluid loss from the burned surface, or locally through restriction from circumferential burns forming localised tourniquets. Fluid loss is directly proportionate to the size of the burn. Fluid replacement formulae are based on burn size. Protein and electrolyte loss can lead to renal failure, as can the subsequent destruction of tissue leading to myoglobinaemia and crush syndrome. Crystalloid infusion should be started as soon as feasible and escharotomies performed to relieve vascular obstruction.

DISABILITY

A quick 'AVPU' before a full examination to assess the burned area and associated injuries is appropriate. Burns are divided into superficial and deep. They are calculated as a percentage of the total body surface. Superficial burns are painful since the epidermis is partially retained and the nerves are intact. With deep burns all the epidermis has gone and the skin will not heal spontaneously. Large burns are treated by grafting, otherwise they will heal with granulation tissue and some epidermal creep from the edges. If the burns are scattered, the size can be roughly estimated in two ways. Firstly, the rule of nines:

• The head and each arm count for 9%.

• The front, back and each leg for 18%.

• The genitalia 1%.

Secondly, the patient's hand is meant to be approximate to 1% of the total body surface area. A more accurate assessment used in hospitals to calculate the area is 'The Lund and Browder Chart' (see Figure Six). It is modified for babies as their heads and trunks are relatively larger.

TRAUMA AND BURNS

Management

Analgesia - Opiates are the drugs of choice and nitrous oxide may be sufficient initially, but it should not be used if there is a risk of inhalation injury, where 100% rather than 50% oxygen is required.

Admission

Those usually admitted to hospital are:

- Patients with burns to problem areas (the face, ears, genitalia or perianal region).

- Adults with more than 15% burns.

- Children with 10% burns or more.

The first two groups usually require plastic and reconstructive surgery. The latter group requires fluid replacement and wound management before later surgery, if required.

Immediate dressings - Wounds should be covered with clean non-absorbent material. Commercial clear-film food wrap laid over the wounds is effective, provided it is not so tight that later swelling will lead to tourniquet effects. Food bags are useful for peripheral limb wounds. Do not apply creams if patients are to be admitted. Small burns can be treated at home with silver sulphadiazine, but this

ESTIMATING THE SIZE OF BURNS

Shade the area of burned skin on the chart. Do **NOT** include simple erythema.
Use the table below to determine the relative body area burned,
dependent on the patient's age.

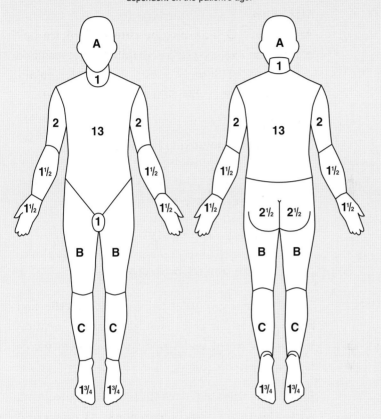

Reproduced with kind permission from Smith and Nephew

Area:	0 yr	1 yr	5 yr	10 yr	15 yr	Adult
A (half of head)	9¹/₂	8¹/₂	6¹/₂	5¹/₂	4¹/₂	3¹/₂
B (half of one thigh)	2³/₄	3¹/₄	4	4¹/₂	4¹/₂	4³/₄
C (half of one leg)	2¹/₂	2¹/₂	2³/₄	3	3¹/₄	3¹/₂

should be avoided on the face since it may lead to a tattoo effect. It is not necessary to give prophylactic antibiotics. Blisters can be left intact to provide a sterile roof to healing burns, but broken blisters should have the dead skin cut away to remove a focus for infection. If infection does occur, dressings should be changed regularly and antibiotic treatment instigated.

ELECTRICAL BURNS

Burns from alternating current are small, but the current passing through the body may lead to ventricular fibrillation and cardiac arrest. The burn may cause deep damage to the tissues. There will also be an exit burn. Such wounds are usually assessed at hospital. Electrical flash burns are caused by the covering of the cable, not by direct contact with the current, and are usually superficial. Direct current is less likely to cause ventricular fibrillation, but high voltage DC current is usually fatal.

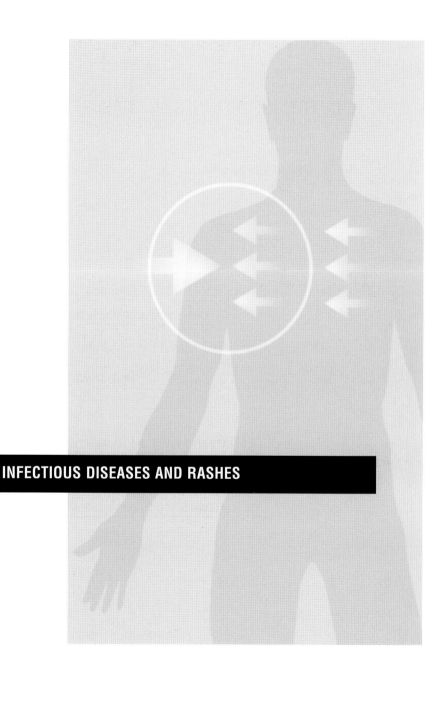

11 INFECTIOUS DISEASES AND RASHES

INFECTIOUS DISEASES AND RASHES

Meningococcal disease

Septicaemia

The immunocompromised patient

Rashes and skin infections

Herpes infections

Travellers' ailments

INFECTIOUS DISEASES AND RASHES

MENINGOCOCCAL DISEASE

Background

Meningococcal meningitis is the most common presentation of meningococcal disease. In around one-fifth of the cases septicaemia predominates; this type carries the highest mortality (15-20% compared with 3-5% for meningitis). Outbreaks occur particularly in the winter amongst children and infants. Vaccines are available against types A and C, but not type B, which is responsible for around two-thirds of outbreaks.

History

There is either a sudden onset of fever malaise and vomiting or a slightly slower onset of malaise, joint pains and photophobia with the typical petechial rash, which initially may be non-specific. There may be history of contact with other cases approximately 48 hours previously. Babies and elderly people may have an insidious onset, but always be suspicious in a patient with vomiting, fever and irritability.

Examination

A photophobic, febrile patient with the classical purpuric rash that does not blanch is associated with the later stages of the disease and needs immediate treatment. Consider this diagnosis in any patient with signs of septicaemia and those with fever and headache who demonstrate signs of meningeal irritation or coma. Babies may have a bulging fontanelle and present with fits.

Management

Any patient in whom you suspect meningitis, unless they have had a previous anaphylactic reaction to penicillin, should be given IV penicillin before transfer to hospital - 1200 mg for an adult, 600 mg for a child of 1-9 years and 300 mg for babies. Arrange transfer to hospital, administer oxygen, and notify the ambulance control that you have a case of suspected meningitis, since they will need to disinfect the vehicle after use.

Subsequent actions

Meningococcal disease is a notifiable disease and telephone contact with the Department of Public Health is essential in order to ensure an effective contact tracing programme. Immediate contacts will be offered prophylactic antibiotic therapy (600 mg rifampicin 12-hourly for 48 hours, with ceftriaxone for pregnant contacts) and immunisation if vaccine is available.

SEPTICAEMIA

This should be suspected in any patient with confusion, hypotension, oliguria and an altered temperature - raised or lowered. The picture is the same whatever the underlying reason, with a massive release of toxins causing collapse and unconsciousness *(see The unconscious patient p.22).* *Toxic shock syndrome* presents with a high fever, erythroderma and is usually associated with tampon use. The diagnosis is made on the history and clinical findings. It is usually due to a staphylococcal toxin but is also seen with streptococci, measles and less common infections. Blood cultures are rarely positive. Hospital management is based on removal of the source (tampons removed and vaginal douching), fluid replacement, pressor agents and penicillinase-resistant penicillin as first-choice antibiotic. The mortality was around 5% in 1989, but has now fallen to almost nil.

There is a toxic shock advice line for patients and information leaflets for the professional provided by TSSTS by telephoning **0171 617 8040**.

THE IMMUNOCOMPROMISED PATIENT

Primary immunodeficiency is rare, but some patients are compromised by medication, such as steroids and cytotoxic drugs, causing them to have an atypical response to infection. Today, the most common cause of compromise is the Aids virus. The immunocompromised patient responds less efficiently to infecting organisms, and to diseases in general, as well as to their treatments. Patients with HIV are often very well-informed about the significance of the disease and their response to illness, and are usually aware of the latest treatments available.

The patient with early HIV infection may present with non-specific malaise, weight loss and lymphadenopathy, and will need differentiating from Hodgkin's disease, other malignancies or TB. The most common infection that results in an emergency is *pneumocystis carinii*, which presents as cough, difficulty in breathing and haemoptysis. Patients with new symptom onset need management of the initial infection in the hospital and subsequent referral to a specialist unit. Known HIV patients may be managed at home with the support of staff from their special unit, with whom the family doctor should liaise. *Pneumocystis carinii* in HIV and other immunosuppressed patients are treated with IV or oral co-trimoxazole (sulphamethoxazole 74 mg/kg/day with trimethoprim 15 mg/kg/day) four times daily.

RASHES AND SKIN INFECTIONS

These always cause alarm but usually are not a true emergency. Often they can be dealt with over the telephone if you are sure the diagnosis is a self-limiting condition. There are some rashes that should command immediate attention – the purpuric rash suggesting *thrombocytopaenia, vasculitis, overdose of steroids* or *meningiti*s and the *acute vasculitis with necrosis* associated with systemic lesions in joints, the gut and CNS. Other rashes are associated with drug reactions, for example fixed drug eruptions with barbiturates.

INFECTIOUS DISEASES AND RASHES

History

Questions should include:

- Where is the rash, when did it start and have you had a similar rash in the past?

- Is it getting better or worse? Does it itch?

- What medication has been tried (by you or your doctor)?

- What else is present – malaise, pain, systemic disturbance?

Examination

Look for systemic upset, toxicity, lymphadenopathy and organomegaly, as well as recognisable exanthemata. The common rashes are:

THOSE ASSOCIATED WITH COMMON INFECTIOUS DISEASES

Chicken pox, German measles (rubella), and measles.

INFECTIOUS RASHES

Erysipelas, impetigo, folliculitis, boils and common children's rashes *(nappy rash, seborrhoeic and atopic dermatitis).*

BODY PARASITES

Body parasites, such as fleas and lice, may present as an emergency, along with the scabetic infestation that results in a widespread allergic reaction.

ALLERGIC REACTIONS

Acute urticaria may be seen as part of a widespread anaphylactic reaction or a milder reaction to an antigen.

HERPES INFECTIONS

HERPES ZOSTER

Herpes zoster may present as an unidentified pain - a rash along the distribution of a nerve or as a partial paralysis. It is a cause of severe pain in some cases and should be watched carefully when the ophthalmic division of the fifth nerve is involved, since corneal ulceration may occur. Good early pain control has been shown to correlate with reduced post-herpetic neuralgia.

HERPES SIMPLEX

Type-one is associated almost exclusively on the face, while type-two causes genital herpes.

Treatment

Herpes zoster does not need expensive antiviral therapy[12] since this has little effect on clinical outcome, but zoster around the eye may be an exception. Corneal lesions should receive topical antiviral treatment in an ophthalmic unit. Topical antibiotic treatments are more likely to cause sensitisation than cure, so systemic antibiotics are not appropriate in infectious rashes.

INFECTIOUS DISEASES AND RASHES

URTICARIA

This depends on the underlying disease. Acute urticaria, like contact eczema, responds well to the sedative antihistamines and removal of the allergen. The causes are legion and urticaria may be recurrent. An allergen is not identified in around 50% of cases, but patients (or parents) should be instructed to keep a diary and identify recurring behaviours or dietary components.

TRAVELLERS' AILMENTS

Patients who develop a fever on return from travel should be assumed to have contracted the disease abroad. They should be questioned about their route and points of touchdown. With patients from malarial areas, assume this is malaria. If prophylactic medication has been taken, then assume it is drug-resistant malaria, usually falciperum malaria. The diagnostic test is a thick blood film for parasitic stain, which can be done in accident and emergency, but the patient with resistant malaria will need admission for medication.

Other fevers include scrub typhus (Malaysia), haemorrhagic fevers, such as lassa fever (equatorial Africa), and fevers associated with the diarrhoeal illnesses.

Diarrhoea may result from the change in environment. If it appears on return from the foreign climate, then it is usually infectious *(see Gastroenteritis and diarrhoea p.99 for differential diagnosis and management)*.

Other travellers' ailments to look out for are the infectious jaundices, (hepatitis A,B and E), helminthic infections, meningoencephalitis, skin ulcers (from leishmaniasis or trypanosomiasis) or itching and skin-swelling (onchocerciasis and loa-loa).

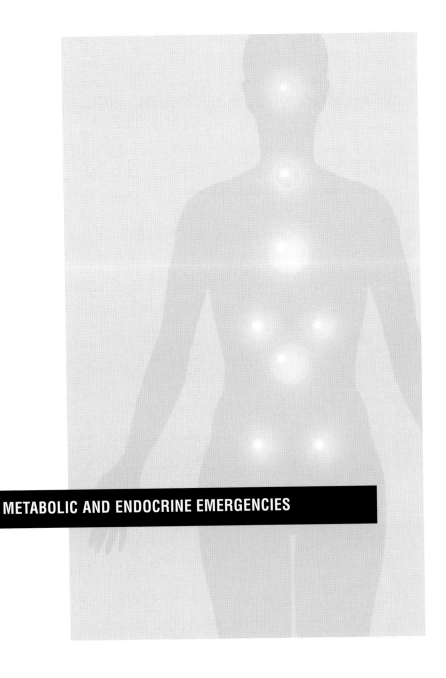

12 METABOLIC AND ENDOCRINE EMERGENCIES

METABOLIC AND ENDOCRINE EMERGENCIES

Metabolic acidosis

Diabetic emergencies

Thyroid disease

Hypothermia

METABOLIC AND ENDOCRINE EMERGENCIES

METABOLIC ACIDOSIS

Background

Although hyperventilation is usually due to anxiety attacks, remember to consider causes of metabolic acidosis which induce a compensatory hyperventilation. These include: overdose of aspirin, ingestion of methanol or ethylene glycol, renal failure and renal tubular acidosis.

History

A firm but reassuring approach needs to be taken to draw out the key features that will differentiate the organic and psychological components. A history of diabetes, renal disease, or a suicide attempt (even a note), will make the diagnosis of an organic cause more likely. Preceding infection, (two or three days of progressive malaise in a diabetic) is strongly suggestive of ketoacidosis, but the absence of this, without a clear history of panic and distress, should indicate the need to visit the hospital.

Examination and management
This will depend on the aetiology.

ASPIRIN OVERDOSE

There may be no specific signs, although the patient may complain of headache or tinnitus before losing consciousness. There may be an obvious suicide note or tablet container. Transfer the patient to hospital as soon as possible. Protect the airway of an unconscious casualty, administer oxygen and keep in the recovery position. Gastric emptying is delayed by salicylate, so admission for gastric lavage is appropriate for up to 24 hours after ingestion. Send any pill containers with the patient, along with the usual referral letter.

INGESTION OF METHANOL OR ETHYLENE GLYCO

Both of these are metabolised by alcohol dehydrogenase, the former to formic acid (via formaldehyde) and the latter to oxalic acid, hence the acidosis. Formic acid leads to blindness, which may preceed unconsciousness, while oxalic acid crystals lead to renal failure. Both methanol and ethylene glycol are taken by alcohol-dependent patients who cannot get any alcohol. The patient may, therefore, present as the stereotypical unkempt alcoholic, which gives another clue in the differential diagnosis. These patients need hospital admission for administration of ethanol, which competitively blocks the ethylene glycol dehydrogenase, thus reducing the production of toxic metabolites.

ACUTE AND CHRONIC RENAL FAILURE

These patients rarely present in general practice as an acute emergency. Existing renal patients have strict guidelines about when to report to their renal unit for dialysis. However, acute renal failure should be considered in an undiagnosed unconscious patient.

DIABETIC EMERGENCIES

Hypoglycaemia is seen most commonly in the patient who has taken their insulin but not eaten, or who has taken an excessive amount of exercise. Such patients usually respond to IV dextrose 50 mg in 50 ml water. Unfortunately, the patient developing hypoglycaemia can become very aggressive, and subtle handling is required to persuade them to take sugar. Once treated the patient usually responds quickly and does not need hospital admission. Occasionally such patients, particularly if they have had a drink, are mistaken for drunks and arrested; therefore, we still see the odd case of the patient who has died of hypoglycaemia while in police custody. Hypoglycaemia accompanying other disorders (for example alcohol excess) also respond to dextrose infusion, but usually in a lower dilution as rehydration is also required.

DIABETIC KETOACIDOSIS

The patient will be flushed with dry skin and may have an accompanying infection. Ketones will be smelled on the breath and detected in the urine, as will raised glucose levels. Although of gradual onset, probably over a few days, there is a risk of deepening coma and death. A general physical examination should be made to ascertain the focus of infection, and blood glucose level should be taken to monitor progress.

Management

There is no immediate requirement to give insulin, but the patient needs admission to hospital for restabilisation. Protect the airway with an oropharyngeal airway and give oxygen. The immediate problem is dehydration associated with the acidosis, so an infusion of crystalloid (a litre of normal saline in the first hour) will start to relieve the metabolic abnormality while awaiting hospital transfer. Although you may have detected an infection, treatment is best left until full assessment has been undertaken in hospital (unless you suspect meningitis).

HYPEROSMOLAR NON-KETOTIC COMA

This is more common in the elderly diabetic who has an underlying infection or malignancy. It develops over a period of time - the sugar reaching into 50 or 60 mmol/l. The comatose patient is hyperosmolar and not ketotic (as the name suggests) and therefore needs immediate admission with IV fluids and 100% oxygen. Even with good care the mortality is around 50%.

ADDISONIAN CRISIS

This is a rare emergency where the patient suddenly loses adrenal function. The patient usually becomes weak and hypotensive, with abdominal pain and vomiting, before becoming unconscious. It is seen classically in the steroid-dependent patient who stops steroid medication or develops an intercurrent illness without increasing the dose. The same

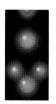

syndrome results from hypopituitarism, but other endocrine deficiencies may be noted. Immediate management requires replacing the steroid deficit with dexamethasone (10 mg IV in the severely ill patient) as this does not interfere with cortisol assays. Transfer for hospital management. *Sheehan's syndrome* is the development of an acute pituitary failure postpartum due to infarction of the pituitary.

THYROID DISEASE

Myxoedema coma usually presents as hypothermia or as a sort of fugue state. Here the myxoedematous fascies will lead you to the diagnosis. The disease has usually taken some time to develop. There is no immediate emergency treatment needed in the community, but the patient should be admitted. *Thyrotoxicosis* may present as an emergency, with diarrhoea and vomiting, tachycardia, fever, flushing anxiety and tremor. Rarely, an acute form occurs, a thyroid storm, where the presenting features are exaggerated and the patient needs admitting to ITU. Elderly people are particularly susceptible to the cardiac effects. Propranolol reduces some of the cardiac effects, particularly the arrhythmia and tachycardia, and should be given IV slowly - 1 mg/kg initially.

HYPOTHERMIA

Background

Not only is this found in people exposed to hostile environments, but it is a common problem in elderly people who may develop it as a primary condition or secondarily through their inability to generate sufficient heat. It also occurs when they become immobile and unable to reach help, for instance, following a fall, a stroke or infarction. Progressive lack of mobility, mental frailty, iatrogenic oversedation and lack of social support contribute to the high incidence rate. Hypothermia is defined as a core temperature of 35 degrees centigrade or below. It is further subdivided into moderate (temperature above 32 degrees) or severe (levels below 32 degrees). Always remember the aphorism: *'A patient is not dead until they are warm and dead.'*

History

The caller may have found the patient by chance and would, therefore, be unaware of the medical history, but the evidence of a fall, self-neglect or chill housing is usually noted. Tablets may be nearby, and the presence of sedatives, cardiac drugs or thyroid replacement therapy should be noted. A history of hypothyroidism or angina is always helpful in discerning a cause, provided you remember that hypothyroidism is often multifactorial.

Examination

Avoid making the patient colder. Keep them covered and examine them area by area. A quick examination, after the ABC of resuscitation, may show the precipitating injury, myxoedematous fascies, or heart failure. Hypothermia is

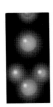

diagnosed by measuring the core temperature with a low-reading thermometer. Rectal temperature is the norm, although aural probes are now being developed. The eardrum temperature closely follows that of the body core. If you have an ECG done, the rhythm will be slow, around 32 per minute, and may show J-waves or arrhythmias. In severe hypothermia ventricular fibrillation is likely to develop, but it is resistant to treatment until the body temperature is raised to above 32 degrees.

Treatment

Severe hypothermia has a high mortality. Avoid unnecessary movement since this may precipitate ventricular fibrillation. Treat the ABCs and give 100% oxygen. Then remove wet clothing and cover with polythene and blankets. Treat life-threatening or very painful precipitating factors immediately, but metabolic problems such as hypothyroidism can be investigated and treated later. Arrange ambulance transfer to hospital.

HYPERPYREXIA

Hyperpyrexia is seen in overdoses of ecstasy and after some anaesthetic drugs. It is also seen in prolonged status epilepticus as a result of continual muscle activity. The patient needs urgent cooling and admission. Chlorpromazine may reduce the heat-producing muscle action of shivering while attempts are made to cool the patient. Tepid sponging and fans are most effective, however do not apply cold water or ice since this produces shutdown of skin vasculature and encourages heat conservation.

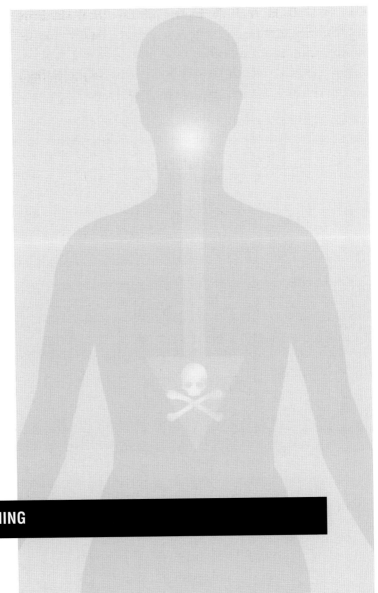

13 POISONING

CHAPTER THIRTEEN

POISONING

Deliberate self-harm

POISONING

DELIBERATE SELF-HARM

Background

Admissions to hospital for self-poisoning represent 20% of acute admissions, and about one-fifth of these need life-support measures in an intensive therapy unit. The death-rate of the in-patient is around 0.6%, whereas the overall mortality is 2%. The poisoning may have been deliberate, accidental or the result of taking recreational drugs. The drugs most frequently used in deliberate self-harm (DSH) are paracetamol, salicylates, narcotic analgesics, tricyclic anti-depressants, recreational drugs and alcohol. Accidental poisoning occurs predominantly in children (household cleaners, garden chemicals and brightly coloured pills left lying around). Carbon monoxide affects whoever is within range.

The aim of management is to restore the patient's physical welfare. The psychiatric assessment is delayed until the patient's mind is no longer under the drug's influence. Accidental poisoning - nearly all in children - usually requires a subsequent assessment by the health-visitor and home safety advice, if not further assessment by a child protection unit.

History

If the initial contact suggests the patient may need resuscitation, then call an ambulance before you visit, and give the caller advice about placing the patient in the recovery position. No further history needs to be taken at this stage, but can be obtained when you reach the home.

Where possible, the initial history should include:

- What has been taken?

- When?

- How much?

- What route?

- Are any other drugs kept in the house / digs etc.?

- Are the drugs still there?
  (If necessary get family or police to search the house)

- Always keep containers.

- Ask about previous suicide attempts or previous accidents and obtain a quick general medical and social history.

- Have there been previous referrals to support services or groups?

POISONING

Examination

All patients should be examined for CNS depression and respiratory or cardiac compromise before specific signs associated with specific poisons are sought. Most poisons cause respiratory depression and slowing of respiration, although organophosphates cause tachypnoea. Pointers to the causative agent may include pinpoint (opiates, organophosphates) or dilated pupils (cocaine, hydrogen sulphide, cyanide). The skin may be sweaty with increased secretions (organophosphates) or cyanosed (methaemoglobin formers such as amyl nitrite). Sometimes skin puncture wounds or traces of ingested substances may be found.

Initial management

The basic principles of poisoning management are:

• The ABC of resuscitation.

• The protection from, and delay of, absorption.

• General supportive therapy.

• Elimination and detoxification.

• Antidotes.

Most treatment is undertaken in the hospital environment. However, we must be able to start appropriate treatment of the patient before they have been assessed and transferred. Basic life support, oxygen administration and simple supportive care will buy time until the ambulance crew arrive. No GP is expected to carry a wide range of antidotes, but in the unconscious patient with respiratory depression, naloxone IV can be effective for more than just opiate intoxication. It should be given in an initial bolus of 400 micrograms, repeated in two minutes if not effective. If this does not reverse the effects, then the causative agent is unlikely to be opiate-related. However, if it is opiate-related, further doses may be required in 15-30 minutes due to the short half-life of naloxone.

When you are concerned about the effects of any drug in overdose, excellent help can be obtained from the National Poisons Information Service (NPIS - *see Appendix*), who have 24-hour doctor-only advice lines. The telephone numbers of the regional centres are given in the British National Formulary.

Subsequent management
The follow-up of poisoned patients need to involve the entire primary health-care team. The long-term effects of the poison may be minimal, but psychiatric assessment and support and risk assessment are mandatory. Health education for parents in cases of accidental poisoning may also be needed. There are many support groups and services for patients who deliberately harm themselves, with or without true suicidal intentions. When more than one case of poisoning raises suspicions of a community incident, GPs should alert the Health Authority so that environmental health advisers can investigate.

14   EMERGENCIES IN CHILDREN

EMERGENCIES IN CHILDREN

Asthma

Choking

Gastrointestinal problems

Urinary tract infections

Child abuse and neglect

Pain relief

Fits

Death of a child

EMERGENCIES IN CHILDREN

Introduction

Children are not just small adults. They have different needs and physiological mechanisms, as well as their own range of diseases. Few general practitioners are experienced paediatricians, but they need to be capable of treating a wide range of paediatric problems in children of differing height and weight. Many interventions and doses are weight-related and one useful tool for the medical management of children is the Broslow Tape. This is a tape developed by an emergency medical physician. It is around 5-feet long and 3-inches wide, with seven coloured sections that list drug doses, equipment sizes, and various other resuscitation and anaesthetic parameters not normally used in general practice. It gives an estimate of weight based on height. Although it tends to underestimate the weight, 80% of Broslow chart estimates are within 15% of the true weight.

The time saved in trying to work out weight and dose in an emergency situation could be far more detrimental than a slight underdosing of the patient, or relying on memory for an infrequently used drug dose. When administering drugs IV, consider diluting for accuracy and then flushing the dose through with normal saline.

Another useful bit of 'emergency' equipment is a small koala bear or other toy attached to your stethoscope; it should win over (or distract) many anxious children.

ASTHMA

Background
Asthma affects around 15% of children under 10 years, 10% of children over 10 and 5% of the adult population. In children it is often misdiagnosed as 'bronchitis'. Be aware of the child with a night cough, or a cough with or without wheeze after exercise and exposure to sudden cold air. Children have a lower respiratory reserve than adults and twice the oxygen consumption per kilogram. They meet increased oxygen demand by increasing their respiratory rate. With children who have pliable chest walls and relatively straight ribs (allowing minimal 'bucket handle' movement and dependence on diaphragmatic movement for gas exchange), there is in-drawing of the whole chest. Children are more likely to develop atelectasis and shunting due to their narrower airways, whose diameter may be reduced by spasm, mucosal oedema and swelling. Infants are obligatory nose-breathers and are easily exhausted by mouth-breathing. Acute asthma in children is still underdiagnosed, often being labelled wheezy bronchitis.

Treatment
As with adults, there is no problem in giving 100% oxygen; indeed it is preferable. If the child is accustomed to using a specific nebuliser, or has one at home, use the one with which they are familiar. Deliver 2.5 mg nebulised ventolin or

100-500 micrograms of ipratropium bromide. If the child is totally unco-operative, then terbutaline can be given s/c 0.1 mg/kg. If there is no response to inhaled drugs, then consider IV salbutamol 5 mcg/kg or aminophylline 6 mg/kg. However, a child this sick needs urgent transfer to the paediatric unit. A recent study showed that children given IV salbutamol early in their treatment (if the first nebulised dose did not induce improvement) recovered significantly more quickly than control.

CHOKING

Background

Small children will put anything into their mouths while investigating their environment and frequently inhale foreign bodies. Any pre-school child with sudden respiratory embarrassment *must* be assumed to have inhaled a foreign body until proved otherwise. Mothers have been taught how to cope with an obstructed airway by the health visitor during pregnancy, since it is unlikely that professional help will arrive in time to save every child. However, in the stress of the moment they may forget. Clear telephone advice from whoever takes the call will be lifesaving, and it is worth having practice reception staff trained to give this advice.

History

On receipt of the call, if there is a clear history of inhaled foreign body, then first-aid instruction should be offered over the telephone while you and/or the ambulance are on your way. However, if there is any chance that the child may have an acute upper respiratory infection with croupy cough and malaise, avoid any airway manoeuvre and visit at once. The oedema of acute epiglottitis may be converted from a partial airway obstruction into a complete block if attempts are made to probe the child's throat.

Management

Complete airway obstruction in a child usually resolves if you undertake immediate resuscitative manoeuvres. Action should be taken immediately, for oedema will soon develop around any foreign body making it difficult to extract. Try exhaled air resuscitation - this occasionally shifts the object into one bronchus, buying time to take the child to hospital. If this is unsuccessful, move on to back blows.

With an infant, place him/her along your thighs, face and head down. Give five firm back blows. This procedure brings gravity to your aid, forcing a shock wave of air past the obstruction. If this does not expel the object, turn the infant over and give five chest thrusts. Alternate these two manoeuvres, checking the mouth in between. After five attempts, give exhaled-air resuscitation.

With a child, bend him/her forward and give five firm back blows. If this does not expel the object, apply abdominal thrusts. Alternate these two manoeuvres, checking the mouth in between. After five attempts, give exhaled-air resuscitation.

If this manoeuvre has not been successful, you will have to make an emergency airway. Place three or four cannulae in the midline between the cricoid cartilage and the thyroid cartlilage - the cricothyroid membrane. This is very superficial, so as soon as air passes through the cannula, do not progress any further. Fix in place with some form of tape and transfer to the hospital as soon as possible.

GASTROINTESTINAL PROBLEMS

Background

Diarrhoea and vomiting are the usual manifestations of most disorders in smaller children, whereas severe gastrointestinal infection, such as *shigella*, may present as high fever and fits before diarrhoea has started. Although electrolyte solutions have greatly reduced admissions to hospital for dehydration, gastrointestinal upset is still the third most common cause for a paediatric admission.

History

A comprehensive history which will commonly differentiate the type of illness includes:

- Dietary intake.

- Changes in powdered milk.

- Contact with other children (particularly toddlers at nursery).

- Family history of upset and travel.

- A routine systemic history.

- Babies in particular need a careful examination to elucidate the cause.

Examination may reveal fever or dehydration and a non-gastrointestinal cause for their diarrhoea, such as otitis media or urinary tract infection (UTI).

Management will depend on the age of the child and the underlying cause, but if there is a diarrhoeal child who is unable to keep down electrolyte solutions, they should be admitted for parenteral rehydration. However, most 'simple' diarrhoea can be managed at home with small frequent feeds of isotonic electrolyte solution. If the case is severe, or if there is more than one case of infective diarrhoea, the Public Health Department should be notified. The local policy for infectious fevers should be followed if there is need for admission.

EMERGENCIES IN CHILDREN

URINARY TRACT INFECTIONS

NEONATAL EMERGENCIES

This is the time when major congenital abnormalities will be found. Usually the patient is in hospital under the care of the neonatologists. The mother who rings in a panic and feels there is a dire emergency has usually found vaginal bleeding. She should be reassured that the mother's raised hormone level has stimulated the baby's endometrium. This is a common, self-limiting problem. Firm reassurance is usually effective.

Neonates may also develop urinary tract infection as part of an overwhelming gram-negative septicaemia from lowered resistance, with few localising signs. Lethargy, vomiting and refusal of feeds (together with a fever and probable dehydration) are the usual symptoms, though not all signs are present in each case and they may be more subtle. The child needs to be in special care and should be admitted immediately, preferably with the mother.

CHILDHOOD

Childhood is the common time for urinary tract infections. Girls have a short urethra, often develop vulvitis and have poor genital hygiene, as well as having underlying congenital urinary tract abnormalities. There is an incidence of UTIs in pre-school children of around 2%, with 10:1 incidence distribution of girls to boys. Once at school the incidence rises to 5% almost exclusively to girls. Renal scarring from vesicoureteral reflux is present in 50% of UTIs under one year, and then becomes less common. Most reflux scarring (previously called chronic pyelonephritis) occurs before the child is 5-years-old and can be reduced by prompt diagnosis and effective treatment.

History and examination may not be as helpful as a mid-stream specimen of urine. Loin pain may be referred, due to ascending infection. Frequency is not always present. Returning to bed-wetting is often significant, as is any vaginal discharge. Younger patients present with non-specific fever, vomiting and malaise rather than focal symptoms. Remember that a foreign body in the vagina may present as a UTI.

Watch body language very carefully when taking the history and performing your examination as this might indicate *child abuse*. Children may wish to ask for help, but they do not have the right vocabulary or courage, so complaining about the genital tract is a way of focusing attention there. If you suspect child abuse then arrange for the child to be seen by a qualified paediatrician. Do not examine the child further, but if you have already started the perineal inspection before the suspicion has been raised, then carefully look for unusual bruising or vaginal discharge without actually touching the area.

Threadworms will cause perivulval, as well as perianal itching, sometimes followed by ascending infection. The infecting organisms are usually from the gut, with E-coli types being the most frequent. Paediatricians differ in their threshold for

investigating children for congenital abnormalities. Nowadays, almost all first UTIs are investigated for underlying congenital abnormalities in an attempt to reduce renal disease. So, treat the initial infection then refer to the paediatrician.

CHILD ABUSE AND NEGLECT

This covers a wide range of abuse, including emotional, physical and sexual. It also includes neglect due to parental drug abuse, failure to supervise, and using the child as a means to attract attention, as in Munchausen syndrome by proxy. Sexual abuse may present with genitourinary symptoms as discussed in the previous section. The physician may note delay in presentation, with physical injury and inconsistency in the history when repeated or given by different narrators.

On examination a general unwholesome appearance may be noted. The child's manner may be abnormal, with little emotional response and wary staring eyes which try to avoid eye contact. Older children will look anxiously towards the carer before answering an apparently simple question. Smaller children will be less active, perhaps hypotonic and present as failure to thrive. The manifestations are legion, but be alert and trust your own judgement when there is the slightest doubt. If the patient is on your own list you may have developmental records; if not, discuss the case with the family physician. If there is time, consider alerting the child protection team through the emergency social worker or police.

PAIN RELIEF

Children need to receive analgesia as suggested in the World Health Organisation pain ladder. This should begin with mild analgesia, then work up through moderate to severe analgesia. However, in emergency situations where there is severe pain, it is reasonable to go straight to opiates. Oral medication needs to be of the appropriate flavour, while avoiding sugar. Consider non-drug therapy too - ice, posture, and elevation of the appropriate part. Strong reassurance is required so that the mother's anxiety is not transmitted to the child, which will encourage the production of pain producing amines.

Children respond well to simple analgesics, such as paracetamol suspension 120 mg/5 ml (dose 10 mg/kg), but this has no anti-inflammatory action. Ibuprofen suspension 100 mg/5 ml (8-10 mg/kg) is equally effective and can be used with minor injuries. If stronger medication is required, then codeine phosphate oral solution 25 mg/5 ml is given (maximum of 3 mg/kg body weight. Recent studies in the accident and emergency journals showed intranasal diamorphine to be as effective as intramuscular diamorphine[13], 0.1 mg/kg for nasal and 0.2 mg/kg for the IM) for the child in severe pain.

EMERGENCIES IN CHILDREN

FITS

As in adults, the mnemonic **'Vowels and Fits'** (AEIOU FFIITTSS) is useful *(see p.132)*, though the emphasis is on different aetiologies, with the febrile fits being the most common. Neonatal fits are often metabolic in relation to low calcium or glucose, whereas childhood fits, particularly in those under four years, are often febrile.

Epilepsy may present at any age in childhood, so all fits need to be investigated by a paediatrician. The emergency management of fits includes: reduction in the fever, medication for control of the muscular movement, and maintenance of tissue oxygenation by giving 100% oxygen. The emergency drug of choice is diazepam which can be given rectally. It comes in preprepared vials containing 5 or 10 mg in solution with a rectal applicator. Rectal diazepam is given in a dose of 0.2 mg/kg, but if you use it intravenously, this should be halved to 0.1 mg/kg.

DEATH OF A CHILD

Most families today are quite unprepared for the death of a child, and health professionals also find coping with childhood deaths very difficult.

Fortunately undergraduate and postgraduate education programmes in breaking bad news and coping with death are widely available. Although these never solve all the difficulties, they provide you with a framework within which to help bereaved families cope with their grief. Remember the many emotional reactions to grief, especially the anger, often directed at the carers and the GP. Be prepared to take this constructively and non-judgementally as a normal part of the grieving process. If you have families from many different cultures, aquaint yourself with their customs so you will not inadvertently cause unhappiness. It is perfectly acceptable to ask about any traditions and the family's wishes.

Deaths in children under one year are usually from natural causes, such as Sudden Infant Death Syndrome (SIDS or 'cot death'), prematurity, congenital abnormalities, or overwhelming infection. The parents may be expecting the child to die, but even so, the event is still a terrible shock. If the child dies in the home, then the death should be confirmed there, and arrangements should be made with the parents as to where they wish the child to be sent. If you are unable to issue a death certificate, then the parents should be told this. They should also be told why the coroner's officer will need to come to the house to talk to them.

In SIDS there is no warning, and the parents must be allowed to come to terms with the bereavement. Be prepared to answer the common questions:

• Was it our fault?

• Was there any pain?

• What do we tell the other children?

• Why?

Often answers are not accepted or not taken in, so the questions recur later. You will probably be asked: 'What happens next?' Ask each parent if they would like to hold the child. They often need permission to do so, but do not push them. Sometimes they may wish to take a photograph or lock of hair, but feel it inappropriate unless the suggestion comes from you. This is more likely with a very young child when there are no existing photographs. Since mothers often come back to ask if there is any visual record of their child, some hospitals take photographs routinely in SCBU. These are subsequently offered to parents at an appropriate moment.

Be familiar with those local undertakers who provide a caring service. They will remove the child to a chapel of rest when the parents are ready to let him/her go. Keep the number of the local police station in your visit bag so you can call the coroner's officer from the patient's home. You may not have much time, but a caring approach, a promise to return, and helping to make arrangements for the bereavement service (or asking a health visitor to call) will all help reduce the family's stress. I always admired a colleague who kept a record of all the deaths in his practice and tried to visit on the first anniversary.

When there is no doubt that the child or infant is dead, it is inappropriate to either initiate resuscitation or to transport the child to hospital, unless the death occurs in the street or after the ambulance service have begun resuscitative manoeuvres. However, if the patient dies in hospital, a later visit to the family is always appropriate.

Sadly, we have to be alert to evidence of non-accidental deaths, and any suspicious circumstances should lead you either to refuse to issue a death certificate or to stall until you have had time to consider all the records. If in doubt, discuss it with your local child protection officer or your coroner's office. Do not delay since evidence may be inadvertently destroyed.

REFERENCES

1. Emergency Care Handbook, NHS 1996. Official Publication of the NHSE.

2. The Labour Party Manifesto. Millbank: London, 1997.

3. Department of Health, Statistics Division. HMSO: London, April 1996.

4. Fry J, Orton P. *UK Healthcare - The Facts.* London: Kluwer Academic Publications, 1995.

5. NHS Executive. Review of Ambulance Performance Standards. Final report of the steering group. Department of Health, 1996.

6. Gentleman D, Teasdale G. Adoption of Glasgow Coma Scale in the British Isles. *BMJ Clinical Research Edition* 1981; **283 (6288)**: 408.

7. Langhorne P. Approaches to the management of acute stroke. *Br J Cardio* 1997; **4**: 97-101.

8. Fennerty AG. The Diagnosis of Pulmonary Emboli. *BMJ* 1997; **314**: 425-9.

9. Little P *et al.* Open randomised trial of prescribing strategies in sore throats. *BMJ* 1997; **314**: 722-7.

10. Marwick C. New Era for Stroke Treatment. *JAMA* 1997; **277**: 199-200.

11. Stiell IG, McKnight RD, Greenberg GH *et al.* Implementation of the Ottawa Ankle Rules. *JAMA* 1994; **271**: 827-32.

12. Helgason HI. Herpes zoster in children and young adults. *Paediatric Infect Dis J* 1998; **17(10)**: 905-8.

13. Wilson JA, Kenall JM, Cornelius P. Intranasal diamorphine for paediatric analgesia: assessment of safety and efficiency. *J Accid Emerg Med* 1997; **14**: 70-2.

A P P E N D I X

NATIONAL POISONS

INFORMATION SERVICES

NATIONAL POISONS INFORMATION SERVICES

BELFAST

The Regional Poisons Information Centre
Royal Victoria Hospital
Grosvenor Road
Belfast BT12 6BA

Telephone: **02890 240503**

BIRMINGHAM

Regional Laboratory for Toxicology
City Road Hospital
PO Box 293
Birmingham B18 7QH

For trace elements Telephone: **0121 554 3801**
For solvents, pesticides, drugs etc. Telephone: **0121 507 4135**

CARDIFF

Welsh National Poisons Unit
Gwenwyn
Llandough Hospital
Penarth
Vale of Glamorgan CF64 2XX

For solvents, pesticides, drugs etc.
Telephone: **02920 711711 ext. 5368 / 5369**

GUILDFORD

Trace Element Reference Centre
Centre for Clinical Science
School of Biological Sciences
Robens Institutes
University of Surrey
Guildford GU2 7XH

For trace elements
Telephone: **01483 879978**

LONDON

Trace Metals Laboratory
Department of Clinical Biochemistry
King's College Hospital
Denmark Hill
London SE5 9RS

For trace elements
Telephone: **0207 737 4000 ext. 4127**

Medical Toxicology Unit
Guy's and St Thomas's Hospital
Avonley Road
London SE14 5ER

GP General Assistance Telephone: **0207 639 9191**
For trace elements and non-biological material Telephone: **0207 771 5372**
For solvents, pesticides, drugs etc. Telephone: **0207 771 5371**

NATIONAL POISONS INFORMATION SERVICES

NEWCASTLE

Analytical Chemistry Unit
Department of Environmental and
Occupational Medicine
Medical School
University of Newcastle
Newcastle-upon-Tyne NE2 4HH

For non-biological material
Telephone: **0191 222 7015** or **0191 222 7255**

SOUTHAMPTON

Trace Element Unit
Clinical Biochemistry Department
Southampton General Hospital
Tremona Road
Southampton SO9 4XY

For trace elements
Telephone: **02380 796237**

INDEX